# They Don't Come with Instructions

## Cries, Wisdom, and Hope for Parenting Children with Developmental Challenges

Hollie M. Holt-Woehl

THEY DON'T COME WITH INSTRUCTIONS
Cries, Wisdom, and Hope for Parenting Children with
Developmental Challenges

All biblical references in this book come from the New Revised
Standard Version, unless otherwise noted.

Cover and interior design: Rob Dewey
Typesetting: PerfecType, Nashville, TN

Print ISBN: 978-1-5064-2741-6
eBook ISBN: 978-1-5064-3418-6

The paper used in this publication meets the minimum
requirements of American National Standard for Information
Sciences — Permanence of Paper for Printed Library Materials,
ANSI Z329.48-1984.

Manufactured in the U.S.A.

# They Don't Come with Instructions

# Contents

# Series Preface

MY MOST sincere wish is that the Living with Hope series will offer comfort, wisdom—and hope—to individuals facing life's most common and intimate challenges. Books in the series tackle complex problems such as addiction, parenting, unemployment, pregnancy loss, serious illness, trauma, and grief and encourage individuals, their families, and those who care for them. The series is bound together by a common message for those who are dealing with significant issues: you are not alone. There is hope.

This series offers first-person perspectives and insights from authors who know personally what it is like to face these struggles. As companions and guides, series contributors share personal experiences, offer valuable research from trusted experts, and suggest questions to help readers process their own responses and explore possible next steps. With empathy and honesty, these accessible volumes reassure individuals they are not alone in their pain, fear, or confusion.

The series is also a valuable resource for pastoral and spiritual care providers in faith-based settings. Parish pastors, lay ministers, chaplains, counselors, and other staff and volunteers can draw on these volumes to offer skilled and compassionate guidance to individuals in need of hope.

Each title in this series is offered with prayer for the reader's journey—one of discovery, further challenges, and transformation. You are not alone. There is hope.

Beth Ann Gaede, Series Editor

## Titles in the Living with Hope Series

*Nurturing Hope: Christian Pastoral Care in the Twenty-First Century* (Lynne M. Baab)

*Dignity and Grace: Wisdom for Caregivers and Those Living with Dementia* (Janet L. Ramsey)

*Jobs Lost, Faith Found: A Spiritual Resource for the Unemployed* (Mary C. Lindberg)

*They Don't Come with Instructions: Cries, Wisdom, and Hope for Parenting Children with Developmental Challenges* (Hollie M. Holt-Woehl)

*True Connection: Using the NAME IT Model to Heal Relationships* (George Faller and Heather P. Wright)

*Waiting for Good News: Living with Chronic and Serious Illness* (Sally L. Wilke)

# Acknowledgments

A PERSON needs love, prayer, support, encouragement, and time to grow and develop. I am grateful for all who have nurtured me to become the person I am. Especially, I am thankful for:

- My husband and pre-editor, Randall; my oldest son, Nicholas, and his wife, Jessica; and my youngest son, Micah. Your love, prayers, and support are invaluable to me.
- My mom and dad, who needed all the above and more to raise me and my sisters, Heidi and Helen, and taught us what it means to be there for each other.
- Friends, special education teachers, medical personnel, and other parents—too numerous to name—who have walked beside me throughout this journey.
- Beth Gaede, book editor, who offered wisdom and guidance and helped me grow as a writer.
- Anne Hokenstad, poetry editor, who offered insight and assistance in a new area of creative expression for me.
- Sue Edison-Swift and Nina Joygaard, who read a shaky draft and offered solid suggestions.
- The parents who participated in the survey, and the parents who wanted to participate but were unable to add one more thing to their schedules.
- The parents who have gone before me on this journey, and the parents who are on this journey now. We are in this together.

Introduction

# If Only Children Came with Instructions

If only children came with instructions
Then parenting wouldn't be so much trial and error,
     and error and trial,
     and more error.

Did I do the right thing?
Handling that problem, I mean, not about having children (Well . . .
   maybe that too . . .)
     Responding to her meltdown?
     Addressing my concerns with the school?
     Challenging him to do more?

When I look back on my days as a parent, none are error free.
     Some days are good.
       Some are a mixture of good and bad.
       Some are just bad days.

If children did come with instructions would I be a better parent?
     Or would I be more concerned about following the instructions
     than loving my child?
       Getting to know her smile.
       Watching actions and reactions.
       Reading his facial cues.

Would I have let my child
     teach me,
     lead me,
     help me,
       to make things up as we went along?

Would I have learned
  to love, deeply love, my child for who she is?
  to find joy, in things big or small?
  to feel pain, in ways I never thought possible, for him?
  to hope for things yet unseen?
  to be challenged beyond belief?
  to still be standing through it all?

Maybe, but maybe not.
Yet, this is my story now,
  still unfolding,
  still progressing,
   I find my way
   as a parent
   without instructions.

—HHW

I OFTEN wished for an instruction book for parenting a child with developmental challenges. I thought it would make the journey easier. When I was pregnant with my oldest son in 1992, my husband and I bought the book *What to Expect When You Are Expecting*. I liked reading it and learning about what was going on in my womb. I read how the baby was developing week by week. I eagerly followed it until my son was born at twenty-five weeks gestation—forty weeks is full term—weighing two pounds, two and a half ounces.[1] I was not expecting that! That edition of the book only had a small section on what could go wrong. We had to put the book aside and make it up as we went along. We had to learn a new vocabulary and figure out what parenting looks like when you are not expecting to be a parent so soon.

Suddenly, we were thrown into the new world of the Neonatal Intensive Care Unit (NICU). What role does the parent play when it takes many doctors, nurses, and support staff to do what would have been done in your womb? We felt like bystanders. We didn't get a chance to hold him until he was two weeks old. After that, we were sometimes told "he is too sick to hold," which goes against a parent's natural instinct when a child is sick. Our baby was in the hospital, and we were commuter parents. I carried a picture of my son in my pocket so I could take him home with me. It was a long 114-day journey of joys, challenges, pain, faith, and hope. When we got him home, we could almost use regular parenting books again.

Two years later, almost to the day, we were back in the same NICU with our youngest son, who was born at twenty-four weeks gestation, weighing a pound and a half, and sicker than our oldest son. That journey was even longer and more extreme than the first. The instruction book we could have written about our first experience was put aside, and once again, we had to make it up as we went.

Our second journey in the NICU lasted 151 days, with one complication after another and seven surgeries. After he came home, the complexities built—failure to thrive—and built—profound hearing loss—and built—autism diagnosis. It was many years before the challenges slowed down and we felt like we got to be "normal" parents again. He is now twenty-three years old. Challenges still exist, but he is further along than we expected or even dared to hope in those early years. No instruction manual could have prepared us.

I have learned over the years that experience is a great teacher. Some of the experiences can be written down. Some cannot. Wisdom and understanding do not come from books alone but from engaging with life and with people. Parenting is a journey of ups and downs, ins and outs. Even if you are prepared in theory, nothing can prepare you for the reality. Parenting is the greatest and most challenging thing most of us do. As parents, we thrive when we embrace the whole parenting journey: the joys, challenges, pain, faith, and hopes.

Parenting is not for the faint of heart. The child's need for food, sleep, attention, safety, health, and love are always foremost in the parent's mind. Decisions need to be made about bedtime, discipline,

> Wisdom and understanding do not come from books alone but from engaging with life and with people.

and education. Factors of each child's temperament, skills, and abilities are to be considered in those decisions. If two parents are raising the same children, then the factors are complicated. How are decisions made? Do we have different roles? What if we do not agree with each other? Another factor that affects parents is the judgment of other people.

Parents are bombarded with judgmental messages from parenting experts about how we are doing too much or not enough for our child. We are judged on how we discipline (or do not discipline), how we support (or do not support), or how we interact (or do not interact) with our children. Parents judge other parents based on our style of parenting, decisions, tone of voice, or choice of clothing. We compare ourselves to other parents, sometimes to make ourselves feel better, "at least I am not like that parent," or to put ourselves down, "I will never be as successful as that parent."

When children have Autism Spectrum Disorder (ASD), Attention-Deficit/Hyperactivity Disorder (ADHD), and/or Fetal Alcohol Spectrum Disorder (FASD), the task for the parent becomes even more complex. Often, the developmental challenges of these disorders create additional stress for parents. Judgments from others and from oneself are harsher, comparisons to parents of neurotypical children increase, feelings of frustration and inadequacy heighten, and a search for help or answers often falls short of expectations. How do we live with both the pain and the joy of raising children with developmental challenges? Like most parents, we deeply love our children and seek to do our best to raise them, but raising children with these challenges is different. It can seem exponentially more difficult. Often, parents feel stretched beyond our abilities.

As a parent who sometimes—no, often—feels stretched, here's something I have noticed that has both an upside and a downside: everyone seems to have advice for parents who are struggling. Even people who have never parented a child will freely offer advice. Sometimes advice is welcome. There is a time and place for advice. But there is also a time and place for simply listening to the parents.

How do we live with both the pain and the joy of raising children with developmental challenges?

Sometimes parents need emotional support, reassurance we are not alone, and a listening, nonjudgmental ear, rather than advice. Parents must continually work on our own emotions and reactions, so we do not place undue burden or strain on the child. We must monitor our own feelings, frustrations, and experiences, so we are able to tend and care for our child. This is tough and lonely work. Sometimes the difficulties get better and sometimes they don't, but most parents get better at handling them.

## Listening to Parents

Over the years, I have met and listened to numerous parents who have children with developmental challenges. As a pastor, part of my role is to listen to the experiences of the people I serve, listening for their struggles and joys, listening for how they sense God is present or how they feel God has abandoned them, and listening for how God's word may comfort or challenge them. As a professor of pastoral care, I have listened to people who live with mental illness and developmental challenges—and their families—and I have taught seminary students to care for all God's children and to foster caring Christian communities. As a parent, I have more than twenty years of lived experience raising my two sons. My youngest son lives with autism and a profound hearing loss. I have listened to parents I have met in support groups, education events, and at school functions.

Throughout this book, my reflections are joined with the cries, wisdom, and hopes of other parents whose children have developmental challenges. Since I have learned and grown from the stories of other parents and value the wisdom and power of personal stories, I designed a survey to invite parents to share their stories and experiences for this book. The survey was sent via a link through personal connections and social media, and encouraged to be shared widely. Fifty-nine parents took considerable time and effort to respond to the survey.

> Sometimes the difficulties get better and sometimes they don't, but most parents get better at handling them.

Many of these parents are raising their biological child, some are raising their adoptive child, and a few are raising their grandchild. Some are new to this journey with their young children—some recently diagnosed—and others have seen their children grow into adulthood. All of us deeply love our children *and* struggle with our children's developmental challenges. We want other people to hear our stories, to listen without judging, and to care without fear or pity.

My intent is not to write a "how to" book on parenting. This book does not offer tips or techniques. This is a book about the experience and the complex internal emotions of being a parent of a child with developmental challenges. My goal is to let other parents of children with developmental challenges know they are not alone, give voice to the often-unexpressed experiences of parents of children with developmental challenges, and offer reflections and insights as a parent, professor, and pastor for parents, family, friends, and members of faith communities.

## What Are Developmental Challenges?

For the purposes of this book, developmental challenges refer to challenges affecting a child's development—cognitive, social, emotional, or physical—caused by Autism Spectrum Disorder (ASD), Attention-Deficit/Hyperactivity Disorder (ADHD), and/or Fetal Alcohol Spectrum Disorder (FASD). While there are many issues or disorders that may cause developmental challenges, these three disorders currently are the most common—ASD, ADHD—or particularly challenging—FASD. Because there are many organizations and resources that focus on each one and can help parents with the details, this book moves beyond the details of childhood disorders and focuses on the experiences of parents.

### *Autism Spectrum Disorder (ASD)*

Autism Spectrum Disorder is a neurodevelopmental disorder, meaning that it is a disorder that affects the development of the

We want other people to hear our stories, to listen without judging, and to care without fear or pity.

Developmental challenges refer to challenges affecting a child's development— cognitive, social, emotional, or physical— caused by Autism Spectrum Disorder (ASD), Attention-Deficit/Hyperactivity Disorder (ADHD), and/or Fetal Alcohol Spectrum Disorder (FASD).

brain. It is called "a spectrum" because it includes a wide range of symptoms, skills, and levels of disability from mild to severe. The broad spectrum of autism makes it difficult for parents, and many other people, to understand the challenges of autism. For example, an individual with mild autism (one end of the spectrum) may be one who would have been formerly identified as having Asperger's syndrome.[2] This person may need a few supports to help them interact socially with others, but they have a normal to high intellect, their traits can help them secure a good job, and they are able to become a self-supporting adult. Individuals with mild to moderate autism (midrange on the spectrum) need social supports and may also have intellectual deficits, requiring lifelong support. While they may never be able to become self-supporting adults, some independence may be achievable. Individuals with severe autism (another end of the spectrum) may have little to no ability to care for themselves or to communicate verbally,[3] and they will always need supportive assistance. For many, their parents are their caregivers.

### Attention-Deficit/Hyperactivity Disorder (ADHD)

Attention-Deficit/Hyperactivity Disorder is also a neurodevelopmental disorder. It is marked by an ongoing pattern of inattention, hyperactivity, and/or impulsivity that interferes with functioning or development. It includes Attention-Deficit Disorder (ADD). Individuals with ADHD often do well as they age and become self-supporting adults. A variety of medications, treatments, and education techniques are available to manage the symptoms. The school years, however, are the most challenging for parents. The heightened levels of activity and the child's difficulty paying attention can interfere with education and relationships.

### Fetal Alcohol Spectrum Disorder (FASD)

Fetal Alcohol Spectrum Disorder "is an umbrella term describing the range of effects that can occur in an individual who is exposed to alcohol during the nine month prenatal period. . . . These effects may include physical, mental, behavioral, and/or learning disabilities with possible lifelong implications."[4] The most severe form is Fetal Alcohol Syndrome (FAS). The range of disorders includes Partial Fetal Alcohol Syndrome (PFAS), Neurobehavioral Disorder Associated with Prenatal Alcohol Exposure (ND-PAE), and Alcohol-Related Neurodevelopmental Disorder (ARND).

Fetal Alcohol Spectrum Disorders are not as common as either Autism Spectrum Disorders or Attention-Deficit/Hyperactivity Disorder. Yet, FASD profoundly affects all aspects of a child's development. Often, an individual with this disorder is unable to gain insight or learn from experience. This creates a perpetual challenge for parents and, depending upon where the individual is on the spectrum, may require a lifetime of support.

### A Word about Diagnoses

Diagnoses are technical descriptions to organize, categorize, and provide consistency. They assist in getting an individual support or access to services or programs, and insurance coverage. Diagnoses ought to be limited to care and treatment, not used to define children. A child is never a diagnosis; they are a living, breathing mystery of life with quirks and a personality, joys and challenges. Outside of medicine and insurance coverage, the diagnosis ought only to be used as a framework for understanding the challenges affecting an individual person. How does ASD, ADHD, or FASD affect them? For instance, if a person has ASD, do they have a preferred way of communication or interaction? Or are there certain situations that increase stress? Getting to know the whole person—the gifts, the personality, the joys, as well as the challenges—ought to be the focus of parents, family members, friends, and members of faith communities.

## Who Is This Book For?

This book is for parents of children with developmental challenges who are seeking encouragement, wisdom, or support. It is also for

A child is never a diagnosis; they are a living, breathing mystery of life with quirks and a personality, joys and challenges.

family, friends, and members of faith communities who want to support children with developmental challenges and their parents.

### For Parents

If you are reading this book as a parent of a child or children with developmental challenges, you may or may not find your experience in these pages. Depending on where you are in your journey, you may find it valuable to jump around to different chapters or specific sections.

- If you are new to this experience, you may want to jump right to the chapter on hope (chapter 8), or you may want to read the reactions of other parents when they received the diagnosis for their child (chapter 1).
- If you have been at this for a while, maybe a certain topic appeals to you, or maybe you are curious to find out if there are other parents who share your experience.

> Be kind to yourself as you engage this book. If a section is difficult for you, leave it. If it doesn't apply, let it go. If it touches you deeply, sit with it.

Just as children with developmental challenges differ from one another, so do the experiences of parents. You may find some experiences or feelings or thoughts are familiar to you. On the other hand, you may find some challenges or joys are unlike your own. You may also find yourself surprised as to how the stories affect you. Whatever the case, be kind to yourself as you engage this book. If a section is difficult for you, leave it. If it doesn't apply, let it go. If it touches you deeply, sit with it. My hope is that you will find support and encouragement in these pages. May you know you are not alone. It is a long and varied journey, and somehow, you will get through it.

### For Family and Friends

If you are reading this book as a friend or family member of someone who has a child with developmental challenges, you will receive a glimpse into raw emotions and seldom-expressed experiences of parents as well as insight on ways to be helpful. Not all people experience the same event the same way. But I hope this book will give you an idea of what your friend or family member may be going through and guide you to offer care and support. What you learn may open an opportunity for a deeper conversation with your friend or family member. For example, if you are wondering about the experience of your friend or family member, you might say, "I read a story about a parent who described their parenting joys, or challenges, as _____. What is it like for you?" Or, simply, "What are the joys or pains you experience as you parent your child with developmental challenges?" If you ask these questions, be prepared to listen and be prepared for raw emotion. Refrain from offering advice or judging. Listening and caring are two important things you can do. If you are interested in helping or supporting, a good follow up question is "How may I help?"

If you think this book might be helpful for your family member or friend to read, be aware that they may or may not be interested. Some parents will welcome the book, read it, and be glad to know they are not alone. Others do not have the time to read a book. Some parents feel the stories of other parents may be more than they can handle at this point in their life. Other parents are tired of hearing other people's stories, because the stories they have heard were not helpful. A mother of child with ADHD, responding to the survey, offered her observation about the value of other people's stories,

> Half the moms on the planet have some horror story about how their son was almost diagnosed with ADHD, but it's just because he was an energetic boy and his teachers didn't know how to handle him, and they were going to put him on medication and screw up his brain, but now he's a rocket scientist/brain surgeon/whatever. Good for that parent's kid! It has nothing to do with your kid, though.

As parents, we never know how our children are going to turn out. It is good to hear stories of hope, but the story may not consider our child and our child's gifts, interests, or abilities. I have noticed that people use these stories to try to make me feel better about my son's future. The truth is I feel a lot better about his future if they get to know my son, care about him, and love him as he is.

If you think this book might be helpful for your family member or friend to read, be aware that they may or may not be interested.

## For Members of Faith Communities

If you are reading this book as a member of faith community, I hope you will learn ways for your faith community to support parents of children with developmental challenges. Many parents of children with ASD and ADHD stop attending worship or do not attend community or social events sponsored by their faith community. The sensory issues, especially sounds, in a faith-community setting can be challenging, not to mention that many community events expect children to sit still and not make any noise. In addition, the parent and the child's week is filled with work, school, homework—which may take many hours—doctor appointments, therapy sessions, and chores around the house, so both parents and children need a break. Sometimes it takes too much effort for a parent to educate a faith community on how to work best with their child. Other books have been written on how to include children with different needs in a faith community and are included in the resource list at the end of this book. My hope is that the stories in this book will move you to listen to the parents in your faith community and help you find ways to embrace, support, welcome, utilize a variety of resources, and engage with parents and their children in a way that will be meaningful for all involved.

## Structure of the Book

This book follows the structure of the online survey I designed for parents of children with developmental challenges.[5] I wanted the questions to cover various aspects of the parenting experience—from their early experience to their joys, challenges, pain, and hopes, to resources and faith, to wisdom they would share with others.

The participants were asked the questions below. The chapter corresponding to each question is noted in parenthesis.

- What did you think and feel when you knew something wasn't quite right with your child but didn't yet have a diagnosis? (chapter 1)

> If you are reading this book as a member of faith community, I hope you will learn ways for your faith community to support parents of children with developmental challenges.

- What did you think and feel when you received the news of your child's diagnosis? (chapter 1)
- What are your joys as you parent a child with Autism Spectrum Disorder (ASD), Attention-Deficit/Hyperactivity Disorder (ADHD), and/or Fetal Alcohol Spectrum Disorder (FASD)? (chapter 2)
- What are your challenges? (chapter 3)
- What causes you pain? (chapter 4)
- What faith resources, if any, have you found helpful? (chapter 5)
- What do you do to take care of yourself? (chapter 6)
- If you were to write an instruction book for family, friends, or faith communities about parenting a child with ASD, ADHD, FASD, what would you include? What do you want them to know? What are ways they might help you? (chapter 7)
- What gives you hope? (chapter 8)

The parents who responded to the survey do not speak for all parents of children with developmental challenges. Nor are the answers from the participants I've included in this book the only answers to these questions. In fact, even the parents who responded may answer the same questions differently at different times in their life—or even different times of the day. The questions in this book are intended to begin a conversation with parents, which I hope can be ongoing, dynamic, and helpful for parents, family, friends, and members of faith communities.

Experience can be a great teacher. May the cries, wisdom, and hope from the parents in this book—and your own experiences—guide you, teach you, offer you hope, and help you to become a better parent, family member, friend, and member of a faith community.

# 1

## Something's Not Quite Right: A Cry for Help

Something's not quite right
    —I cannot identify it.
I sense in my gut something
    and I cannot find the words.
Is it me? Or it is my child?
It must be me.
What I am doing wrong?
I followed the expert's advice
    —it didn't help
I feel like a failure as a parent.

Something's not quite right
What is it?
    —I cannot identify it.
I want to ask for help
    and I am afraid.
Am I more afraid to find
    something is wrong with me
    or with my child?

—HHW

## In the Beginning . . .

WHEN DO you know something isn't quite right with your child? Sometimes you come to know things are not quite right through an unfolding process. You notice little things, a reaction that seems a little off or an action that seems odd. Slowly these things add up and you begin to wonder if something else is going on. Sometimes it is an event, a major outburst, or a violent behavior. Whatever the case, it is a significant part of the lifelong journey with children with developmental challenges.

The journey with our son was so complicated at the beginning, it was tough to sort out which issues were from his feeding difficulties—he was orally averse[1] and exclusively tube-fed for eighteen months—and which issues were from the premature birth. We knew it was common for children born premature with numerous complications to have developmental delays, and we were told his oral aversion might be delaying his speech. We didn't even consider he might have a hearing loss until two people in one week asked if he had had a recent hearing test. He was three years old. That "coincidence" aligned with something inside of us that we sensed wasn't quite right. We followed up on this with our pediatrician and had his hearing tested. We learned he had a severe to profound hearing loss in the high frequencies, and he was missing 80 percent of all language. We felt awful! How could we miss that?

Early on in the journey of children with developmental challenges, it is common for parents to blame ourselves for anything that isn't quite right with our child. We think we are failures as parents, or bad parents, or that we are doing something wrong. One mother of a young daughter with ADHD summarized the struggles of this time for parents, "I was frustrated, worried that I had been parenting wrong—that it was somehow my fault. Wondering if it was my imagination—was I making something out of nothing? The guilt part was the worst, though." Puzzlement, frustration, worry, blame, wondering, guilt, and more swirl through the mind of parents in the beginning.

*Puzzlement*

The first survey question was "What did you think and feel when you knew something wasn't quite right with your child, but didn't

> Early on in the journey of children with developmental challenges, it is common for parents to blame ourselves for anything that isn't quite right with our child.

yet have a diagnosis?" Many parents expressed their puzzlement early on in their journey.

One mother replied that other people "kept saying [my children] were late bloomers. But you know in your gut something is wrong." The "gut" experience is difficult to describe, and it is different for each person. For instance, I cannot tell you exactly what it was about those two inquiries to have our son's hearing checked that seemed to resonate with us. I think this "gut" feeling comes from watching minute details of your child—facial expressions, body language, tone of voice, interactions with you and others—and getting to know their personality.

Often, parents don't have any idea how to make sense of the situation. One couple stated that they "were baffled. [Our son] was and is *so* bright and articulate. He doesn't fit with what is expected of him." Their son's abilities were not lining up with their expectations, and therefore something was not right. Another mother responded to the survey question,

> I wasn't sure what was wrong. Both of my boys have ADHD, so I had nothing to compare to (i.e., a neurotypical child). I grew up with only sisters; we thought they were just active boys. However, my boys were more active and intense than many other children their age.

Many parents of children with ADHD struggle to determine what is "normal" activity for a child. Parents are also aware of some of the current debates about ADHD—for example, that it is over diagnosed or over medicated[2]—so as parents we try to convince ourselves that something is wrong with us, not the child. Another mother described her early experience and struggle in detail,

**Many parents expressed their puzzlement early on in their journey.**

With my son who has ADHD, it was so frustrating because we assumed he was just rambunctious, and there's so little support. There's the assumption that your kid is just bad, and there's so much negativity about the very idea of ADHD that even mentioning "I think my son has ADHD" to certain friends would lead to a tirade about how ADHD is so over diagnosed, and the school system really just hates boys—even though none of the other boys in his class had this many problems—and ADHD is just another term for "being a boy," etc., etc., etc. It's strange to me; my options were (A) my child has a treatable neurological condition, (B) my child is just a chronically misbehaving kid and there's nothing anyone can do about it except pray he doesn't end up in prison, or (C) I'm a lousy parent who can't control my kid. Yet for some reason, people wanted to reassure me that A was the one that wasn't the case! I desperately wanted a diagnosis for him because it would show that it really *was* something outside anyone's control.

The internal dialogue for each parent is different, but many experience this back-and-forth wrestling between blaming it on ourselves and wanting the problem to be something outside of our control.

### Frustration

The most common experience at the beginning of the journey with a child with developmental challenges is frustration. Parents experience frustration with the child's behaviors and with the repeated failed attempts to find something that helps us work with our child. Or we experience frustration with how long it takes to get information that will help us and our child. We want answers. We want to know what's going on and what we can do about it, but it takes time to find the right people or professionals who will listen to our concerns and help us help our child.

Scheduling appointments, administering tests, and waiting for results takes a long time. After all that, the professionals still may not be closer to figuring things out, or the parents may have to start over again with another set of professionals. Frustration often builds

The most common experience at the beginning of the journey with a child with developmental challenges is frustration.

For some parents, frustration was accompanied with the feeling of being alone.

Not only the challenging behaviors but the search for answers can be physically and emotionally exhausting.

during this time and is sometimes accompanied with feelings of inadequacy, helplessness, embarrassment, and not being heard. One couple reflected, "[We] began to feel defeated because we didn't know what to do to stop his outbursts." If professionals don't know what is going on, what are the parents to do?

For some parents, frustration was accompanied with the feeling of being alone. One mother of a teenage daughter with ASD said, "[We were] frustrated that we weren't landing on a diagnosis that could get her the help she needed. We always felt a little bit off the beaten path and found it hard to relate to other families." This image, "off the beaten path," is apt. Imagine following a path well worn by numerous travelers. Then slowly the path becomes less and less discernable. The direction is not clear. You have to make your own path, even if you are not sure where you are going. If there are other travelers on the path, they might not be there at the same time as you, or they might be going in a different direction, or they might be just as lost as you. Wandering in a new terrain without direction can be scary and stressful. This image of "off the beaten path" highlights the feeling of being alone on the journey, of crying out and not being heard.

### Other Feelings

The depth and breadth of other feelings were expressed by one mother: "I felt like my world was out of control, and I felt often like I was a bad parent. I couldn't seem to get a handle on my son's behavior. My husband and I were exhausted." Not only the challenging behaviors but the search for answers can be physically and emotionally exhausting. It takes energy to keep searching when you know something isn't quite right. Another parent was "exhausted from trying to get help, but no one seemed to see what I experienced." How long do you keep searching? Just because no one else understands doesn't necessarily mean it doesn't exist. Where do you start? Where do you go next?

Parents may feel anxious during the early days, especially as we seek information about what may be causing the developmental challenges. But possessing knowledge often is not enough to dispel the anxiety of the situation. One parent, who had a prior career in elementary and early childhood education, said, "I started asking about autism when my son was three. It made me anxious." Parents might be worried about the child, scared the challenging behaviors will never end, or worried whether we will be able to help our child. As one mother said, "I wondered what was wrong. It was so stressful. I wondered if it would [always] be this way."

Parents may be confused, lost, guilty, scared, overwhelmed, and conflicted during this time. The complexity of emotions and the stress of the situation can cause a lot of disruption in every aspect of the lives of the parents and families. Jobs may be disrupted with calls from the school or with visits to doctors and specialists. Sleep may be disrupted with worry or by a child's sleeping difficulties. Thoughts may be disrupted by wondering what to do next or what will happen next. Eating habits or exercising may be disrupted by the amount of time it takes to care for the child. Social events or other responsibilities may be disrupted by a child's behavioral issues.

> Parents may be confused, lost, guilty, scared, overwhelmed, and conflicted during this time.

## What Can We Do?

Sometimes a parent needs to express frustration, anger, or anxieties and have someone listen. Other times a parent needs someone who will be willing to go along on appointments or to help us think about what else we could do. The information received in the beginning of this journey can be overwhelming. Having someone else along to hear what is being said, write it down, or even to ask clarifying questions can help parents process the information. I remember many visits with doctors where I hardly heard anything after the initial shock of the news. When we were in the NICU, the doctor talked with us while the nurse was present. After the doctor left, we would ask the nurse to repeat—over and over again—what was said until we understood. Sometimes there is just too much information, or the language is to technical to process all at once, and it takes time and repetition to understand.

Where does a parent go if we feel something isn't quite right with our child? Often the starting point is the family doctor or pediatrician. If the doctor is not helpful, a referral to see someone else can be requested. The referral can be for someone in the same clinic or elsewhere who may specialize in working with children who have challenging behaviors. Some school districts have helpful programs, like early childhood intervention and special education, and social workers to navigate families toward assistance for their child. Some organizations, like The Arc, offer a variety of services and programs for families and people with intellectual and developmental disabilities.

Friends or family members can often be helpful during this early discovery stage by offering support and encouragement. Family members and friends can acknowledge the struggle, listen, and ask for, as well as offer, specific ways they can help. For example, they may volunteer to go along on appointments, cook meals, or provide childcare for the other children while the parents go to appointments or go out on a date.

> Family members and friends can acknowledge the struggle, listen, and ask for, as well as offer, specific ways they can help.

Prayers can be a powerful, meaningful, and helpful support for parents and children. Friends, family members, or members of faith communities may offer to pray with or on behalf of parents and our children. Three times other people prayed for me and my family stand out in my memory. One time was when my oldest son had a febrile seizure at eighteen months old. The seizure caused him to aspirate and develop pneumonia. He needed to be airlifted from the local hospital in the rural area where we were living at the time to a more specialized hospital. Four pastor colleagues who were in my text study group came to join us at the local hospital. After our son was placed on the helicopter, they placed their hands on us and prayed. We felt empowered by the care of their presence, the words of their prayers, and the warmth of their touch.

Another time other people prayed for us took place while my husband and I were at a church conference. Our youngest son was eight weeks old and still in the hospital. He had stabilized enough for us to attend the three-day conference seventy minutes away from the hospital. Suddenly, he took a sharp turn for the worse and needed emergency surgery. We gave permission over the phone and quickly left the conference to drive to the hospital. Later, we were told that the bishop led the whole assembly in "a very moving" prayer for us and our son. The fact that the bishop interrupted the meeting and 785 other people joined with him to pray for us was humbling and meaningful.

The third prayer event took place at another time when our youngest son was hospitalized and very sick. Our son's attending nurse, knowing we were people of faith, prayed with us next to our son's bedside while the doctors were fervently working on him. Her prayer for us and with us at that time reminded us we were loved and cared for by her, by the hospital staff, and by God.

As I reflect on these events, over twenty years later, what made these times of prayer powerful, meaningful, and helpful was the relationship each of the people who prayed had with us and the relationship they had with God. Neither my husband or I remember exactly what was said, nor were we even present for one of those prayers, but I do know that those times of prayer were profound for us and continue to be as we look back on them. Prayer is a mystery of faith; I don't know exactly how it works. I do know that God works through prayer in ways I will never understand.

Members of faith communities, be mindful that the journey of the parents of children with developmental challenges may be long, and parents may need encouragement to remember that God has not forgotten us. In the Scriptures, there are many stories of long journeys where God provides for God's people—Abraham and Sara, Jacob, Joseph, Hannah, Ruth, Elijah. When God's people wandered in the wilderness for forty years after the exodus from Egypt, God supplied water, manna, and quail daily to give God's people strength for the journey (Exod 15:22–16:35).

These stories ought to be recalled in ways that will encourage, not discourage the parents. For example, the extended wandering in

> Prayer is a mystery of faith; I don't know exactly how it works. I do know that God works through prayer in ways I will never understand.

the wilderness is a particular story that details the failings of God's people and God's response. Placing blame on parents for our child's developmental challenges, by saying that God gave us this child to test us or because we weren't trusting God, is wrong and unhelpful. My training and faith convince me that God does not "give" certain illnesses, situations, and challenges to test people. I believe we live in a broken world with pain, suffering, and challenges.

As a Christian, I believe God enters this world through Jesus Christ to walk with us, to strengthen us and help us to face life in this broken world. By going through difficult challenges, we may *feel* tested or punished, but God has not forsaken us (Deut 31:8, Matt 28:20). We may learn through this experience, but God doesn't "give" us these things to teach us a particular lesson. I had people tell me that God "gave" me two premature births to teach me some lesson—they usually supplied what it was I needed to learn. I responded saying, I have learned a lot of different things through these experiences, but God could have taught me those lessons in another way. I may or may not find a way to make the experience mean something to me. However, that is for *me* to discern. For me, it is helpful to know that no matter what I experience, God feels my pain, hurts with me, and walks with me on the unfamiliar journey. I have always found the words of Isaiah comforting:

> When you pass through the waters, I will be with you;
> and through the rivers, they shall not overwhelm you;
> when you walk through fire you shall not be burned,
> and the flame shall not consume you. (Isa 43:2)

The passage says *when* not *if*. Challenges will enter our lives, even the lives of people of faith, and when they do God will be with us.

## Turning the Corner

In all journeys, there comes a time when the corner is turned, and the earlier difficulties become easier to manage. Sometimes it comes quickly, other times it may take a while. A day does come where

Challenges will enter our lives, even the lives of people of faith, and when they do God will be with us.

the intensity of the early thoughts and feelings begins to subside as both parents and children begin to deal with the realities of the diagnosis, gain some new skills, and adopt new approaches. Since human brains are growing and developing until about twenty-four years old, behaviors or even diagnoses may change as the child ages. But even so, there comes a point where there is more known than unknown, more information is gathered, and parents better understand our children and how to help them.

One mother welcomed her opportunity for turning the corner:

> At first, with my daughter on the [autism] spectrum, I was in denial. I knew something wasn't right, but I kept assuming it was just a developmental delay, particularly because girls present so differently from boys. She was extremely rigid in her play and she had trouble stringing more than two or three words together, but she was friendly, cheerful, and craved affection; that meant she wasn't autistic, right? And "autism" is so much scarier a word than it needs to be. As it became clearer to me that her symptoms put her on the spectrum, though, I wanted a diagnosis very badly. If she really did have autism, we would know why she acted the way she did, and we would have a whole new toolbox with which to tackle it.

My son was diagnosed with autism when he was six years old. I found the autism diagnosis helpful. I had been noticing some things for a while—his lining up toys in a certain way, sorting toys by color, and vigorous rocking motions. I remember after getting the diagnosis talking to a neighbor. My son was pushing his stroller in circles in the driveway—a repeated pattern of behavior is a common trait of autism—as I was explaining to my neighbor what we had learned. He said he couldn't believe it. Our son seemed normal to him. My son continued pushing the stroller in circles for at least ten minutes. Many people have a certain stereotype in their mind of autism and do not understand the wide spectrum of autism disorders. Even our pediatrician couldn't believe our son was on the autism spectrum because our son could engage with people. Not everyone will understand what the diagnosis means or how it

In all journeys, there comes a time when the corner is turned, and the earlier difficulties become easier to manage. Sometimes it comes quickly, other times it may take a while.

may be helpful. For me, the diagnosis helped me understand my son better and find ways to help him.

At some point, parents realize that our child's developmental challenges require a new or different approach or, as the mother above said, "a whole new toolbox"—new tools and techniques to add to our repertoire of responses. With the journey of discovery mostly completed, parents have a better idea what is going on with our child and how we might proceed. One parent shared her inner struggle after the diagnosis,

> Ok, but isn't ADHD over-diagnosed? Do I really want to medicate my child? Still not sure the whole thing isn't just because I'm "doing it wrong!" Then I decided that if the meds could help her, why should I keep them from her? Didn't that also make me a bad mom? So, ok. Let's try the drugs and see if they help. They did. The reports back from teachers made me cry with relief.

After receiving the diagnosis, parents experience a range of thoughts and feelings: relief, sadness, grief, a mixture of emotions, and resolve.

### Relief

More than half of the parents in this survey responded with relief to the diagnosis. The relief came from identifying what was causing the issues or behaviors and getting the tools to help their child. The diagnosis did not solve all their challenges, but it helped the parents know that the experiences with their child fit a pattern. One mother described her mixed emotions this way:

> It all fit together, and we finally had more info about why our child reacted to some things the way she did *and* now had tools to help her! It was a relief, but I felt horrible that it took us so long to get a diagnosis when she could have received help sooner.

Parents often expressed regret about not having a diagnosis sooner. But even with the long journey, and sometimes misleading or changing information, they were still relieved. One mother stated,

---

After receiving the diagnosis, parents experience a range of thoughts and feelings: relief, sadness, grief, a mixture of emotions, and resolve.

The diagnosis did not solve all their challenges, but it helped the parents know that the experiences with their child fit a pattern.

"My son was under-diagnosed for many years, so it was a relief to finally receive a full and proper diagnosis." Another mother described her long journey:

> Every time I'd asked, my concerns had been dismissed—by two different school psychologists, a neurologist, and a developmental pediatrician. When my son was eight, his pediatrician diagnosed him with ADHD. It took two more years before anyone heard my concern and told me where to go for neuropsychological testing to identify Autism Spectrum Disorder (Asperger's Syndrome).

Despite her long journey, this mother was relieved when her son finally received a diagnosis for ASD.

When parents have more than one child with developmental challenges, they may experience different emotions, depending upon the diagnosis or whether the child was the first or second to be diagnosed. One parent responding to the survey, who has a daughter and a son with ADHD, said she was "surprised the first time, relieved the second." A mother of two daughters said that "with ADHD it was relief, with ASD it was like preparing for a triathlon." Another mother, who has a daughter diagnosed with ASD and a son with ADHD, had a similar reaction,

> I had mixed feelings about my daughter's autism diagnosis. At first, I was relieved because it explained so much; then I cried because I was so worried that we'd never be able to help her live with her autism, or that she'd be bullied in school. With my son (ADHD), it was pure relief. It explained so much about his behavior and it meant that we could get his IEP [Individualized Education Program] adjusted to reflect the fact that he really did have a reason for acting the way he did.

When the unknown is known, often the burden is eased. For me, when I do not know what is going on, I can imagine perils much worse than reality. However, when I have a framework of what to expect, I find focus and direction. Even though the challenge is there, I have some idea of what to expect, and I can focus on what the situation requires.

The reality of the situation is that even though many parents experience relief when we know the diagnosis for our child, we still have a child with challenging issues. Ultimately, this leaves many parents experiencing mixed emotions concerning the diagnosis. One grandparent said she felt relieved to have answers, but now she wondered, "how would we deal with all the difficult behaviors?" One mother described her response to the ADHD diagnosis of her son this way:

> I had mixed feelings. On the one hand, it felt like there was finally some hope. With a diagnosis, we knew what we were facing. I knew that there were medications and therapists that could help us. On the other hand, I also had worked with many kids with ADHD professionally. I knew there would be challenges. In some ways, I grieved that my son was one of "those" kids.

Parents may express many emotions upon receiving our child's diagnosis. Most parents are relieved. We are relieved to have a better idea of what to expect with our child and what we can do. However, parents may feel sadness or grief upon receiving the diagnosis. The long process to get a diagnosis is over, but we are still dealing with our child's challenging behaviors along with our own puzzlements, frustrations, worries, and fears.

### Sadness

Sadness and grief are very close to each other. Sadness is an emotion that may be caused by grief, and grief is an experience of loss often expressed by sadness. Most people think of grief as the response to death. Grief is experienced at times of any loss. In addition to death, grief can also be triggered by the loss of dreams and expectations.

A woman shared her first reaction to receiving her grandson's diagnosis: "Was I capable of caring for this child? It would be a difficult challenge." She experienced loss of confidence and maybe

The reality of the situation is that even though many parents experience relief when we know the diagnosis for our child, we still have a child with challenging issues.

the loss of her expectation as a grandparent. Many parents in this survey mentioned they were disappointed, devastated, heartbroken, or sad after learning of the diagnosis of their child.

The loss of dreams or expectations and the sadness one experiences are real. Often, it is helpful for parents to acknowledge this sadness and express the grief about what we have lost. What makes expressing grief a challenge for parents is that we feel bad about being sad. Not many people understand the odd complexities of this grief. For example, I grieved the loss of a full-term pregnancy. I had two pregnancies and two premature births. I never looked pregnant, and both deliveries were by caesarian section. It sounds odd to say that I wanted to experience the discomfort of my belly stretching out to expand with my growing baby, being unable to see my feet, having a natural childbirth, holding my child immediately after birth, and taking my child home the next day. When I have expressed this grief, people have responded, "Well, you should be happy you have two children." I am glad I have two children. I am not grieving my children or their lives. I grieved the loss of a full-term pregnancy experience. Mothers who have experienced the discomforts of a full-term pregnancy have told me that I didn't miss much, but I still would have traded all those months in the NICU in a heartbeat to have a full-term pregnancy.

Grieving is part of the experience of having children with developmental challenges. Parents need the space and time to grieve the loss of expectations and dreams. Some parents may grieve and express a sense of loss more than others. To work through grief, I believe it is helpful for the person to acknowledge the reality of the loss, experience the pain, adjust to the new reality, and find a way to honor that loss while still moving forward.[3] This will look different for each person.

Acknowledging the reality of the loss may be as simple as saying, "I miss the 'typical' challenges of being a parent," or noting that your child will not develop at the same rate as their peers. Experiencing the pain means that it is okay to be sad, and there are days when

Grief is experienced at times of any loss. In addition to death, grief can also be triggered by the loss of dreams and expectations.

the pain is greater than others. The challenge is to not cover up the pain with distractions, numb it with substances, or convince yourself you shouldn't be feeling this way. To work through grief includes adjusting to the new reality. That takes time, effort, and patience. Early in the journey, parents may feel unable to adjust, but it will happen. I found that if I took it one step at a time, and gave myself time to learn each new skill, I was able to adjust. While working through the grief, parents also find a way to honor the loss and resolve to move forward.

*Resolve*

One mother used three words to express her feelings and her internal process when she received her son's diagnoses of ADHD: "conflicted, afraid, resolve." After the initial reaction, many parents resolve to accept the diagnosis and move forward to help their child. When another mother learned of her toddler's autism diagnosis, she was ready to move forward with "clear direction, inspiration, and motivation." One parent "was relieved to finally have an answer. Something I could look up to learn more." Another father resolved to get "some information to go forward for help."

With the search for answers complete, or mostly complete, parents are ready to move forward to help our children. We gather new tools, sharpen old ones, throw out the ones that are not helpful, and customize our tool kit to help raise our children with developmental challenges.

## Grace for the Moment

Now that the journey of parenting a child with known challenges has begun, many parents may wonder, "how will I get through it?" I know I have asked myself that question more than once over the years. I look back on all that we have gone through and all the challenges, both expected and unexpected, that we have faced. As a person of faith, I believe God has given me grace for the moment when I needed it and the ability to get through it.

The challenge is to not cover up the pain with distractions, numb it with substances, or convince yourself you shouldn't be feeling this way.

When I was about to leave my job as a pastor and begin my PhD studies, my husband and I decided to do a few things while we still had money—to make some home repairs and go to Sea World. The trip to Sea World was pricey for us, but it was something I wanted us to do as a family. We found a coupon for five dollars off entry into the park and prepared for our trip. On the day of our Sea World adventure, we arrived before the gates opened to get the most out of our day there. We parked the car, and as we were unloading the stroller from the trunk, a woman approached us and asked if we had tickets. I told her we didn't, but we had a five-dollar-off coupon. She replied that she had a season pass with tickets for guests to enter with her for ten dollars apiece, and it expired that day. She didn't have anyone who could use the tickets, so she offered them to us. Stunned at our good fortune, we followed her through the entrance. We paid less than half of what we would have without her. We thanked her and never saw her again.

It wasn't until we had already committed and were about to enter the park that this woman showed up and provided for us. She didn't show up weeks earlier while we were planning the trip. She showed up at the time we needed it. For me, that incident became an example of God providing and giving us the grace we need, when we need it, not before—which is really when I want it, and the earlier the better. Throughout the years, there have been many moments of grace when we have received what we have needed at the time we needed it to face struggles, tense moments, or challenges. I have often felt unprepared for many of these experiences, but I have received grace for the moment to get through them.

Grace for the moment, for parents, can be new technology or techniques acquired at the right time, or having a friend call or text for no particular reason. Family and friends have often offered us God's grace for the moment. While emergency hospitalizations are never planned, we have always had family or friends offer extra support and prayer during those times to help us get through. Grace for the moment can be experienced by family, friends, and members

As a person of faith, I believe God has given me grace for the moment when I needed it and the ability to get through it.

of faith communities at all times, as they reach out to care, pray for, and support parents of children with developmental challenges.

## For Reflection and Discussion

1 What did you think and feel as you read this chapter?

2 What surprised you as you read this chapter?

3 Describe a time when you experienced "grace for the moment."

4 (Parents) What kind of support would be helpful for you? Who are people who you can ask to help or support you? What prevents you from asking for help?

5 (Family or Friends) What did you learn from this chapter that may help you support or care for parents of children with developmental challenges?

6 (Members of Faith Communities) What Bible stories or Scriptures come to mind in which God offers support during a long journey or long struggle? How might these stories or verses be used to encourage parents?

# 2

## Down in My Heart: A Cry of Joy

As I child, I learned a song
"I've got
    Joy, joy, joy, joy
        down
        in my
            heart."

As a parent, I discovered joy
    near the top
        of my heart
            in my child's smile
            while a new thing—big or small
                was accomplished.

As a guardian, I measured joy
    in the caverns
        of my heart
            a meltdown—one minute
                shorter than the last
            a trip to the store—nearly
                five minutes
                    a success.

As an adult, I found love
    for my child
        encompassing my heart
            heart-filling joy
            keeps-me-going-in-tough-times joy

Child of mine, as your parent,
    "I've got
        Joy, joy, joy, joy
            down
                in my
                    heart."

—HHW

JOY IS more than happiness. It carries with it a sense of delight, celebration, or something that lifts your spirits. Happiness is fleeting; it is an emotion that comes and goes. It doesn't have staying power. Joy might include happiness, but it is deeper and lasts longer.

If you were to ask a parent of a child with developmental challenges, "Are you happy?" my guess is that none of us would say we were happy about our situation or the challenges we experience. With the stress and difficulties of parenting children with developmental challenges, there are also days when joy is absent. Often, many days pass before we experience a moment of joy with our children.

There *are* joys, however, even when parenting children with developmental challenges. Sometimes we must look harder to find these joys, but joy can be found even in the most challenging situations.

I have experienced great joy as a parent. One of my joys was coming home from work when my children were young and hearing them shout, "Mama's home!" Then they would proceed to tell me about their day or show me something they had made or discovered. I enjoyed watching them learn, grow, and develop at every stage along the way. As young adults, they still fill me with joy when we talk or spend time together.

Some experiences of joy will be simple, others profound, but as we speak about our children, you will see a smile on our face or a twinkle in our eye. If you give us time, some of us will tell you

Joy can be found even in the most challenging situations.

more than you want to hear, but we will share with love, joy, and excitement.

In the survey, I asked "What gives you joy as you parent a child with Autism Spectrum Disorder (ASD), Attention-Deficit/Hyperactivity Disorder (ADHD), and/or Fetal Alcohol Spectrum Disorder (FASD)?" For the parents in this survey, many of their joys are the same as other parents, as one mother replied, "seeing the excitement on their faces for little things, like going bowling or to McDonalds." However, some of their joys are unique, like the joy of the woman who feels delight "when [my children] can manage their anxiety and depression and get through the day."

## Finding Joy

Finding joy requires stopping to reflect on the joy in your life. It may require setting aside frustrations or struggles and focusing on the child. The parents in this survey found joy in their child, in accomplishments, and in the gifts or qualities of their child. Some even found joy in the unique traits of ASD or ADHD.

### Joy in the Child

Many parents responded that they received joy in their child—how their child engaged with their environment or played or interacted with other children. One mother found joy in her daughter's joy. Other parents replied,

- "I love being part of my daughter's life—seeing her grow and learn and love and laugh! Hearing how she delights teachers and other adults—watching her play with other kids. I especially like seeing her help younger or less experienced kids."
- "I can still remember [my son's] exuberance when he first saw Christmas tree lights. He did a dance of joy."
- "Enjoying whatever she can enjoy: characters, costumes, theater, running, traveling, or special events."
- "He's my beloved, beautiful, intelligent, creative, loving child, no matter what."

> Finding joy requires stopping to reflect on the joy in your life.

Children with developmental challenges may not interact with other people very well. When children make progress in social skills, or as they grow in other skills leading to adulthood, it is a joyous time for a parent. One mother of three adopted children with ADHD stated that for her, "watching them develop into people that folks like to interact with is a huge joy."

When children experience developmental delays, developments that other parents take for granted can bring joy. A mother of a toddler diagnosed with ASD delights in "every smile, hug, kiss" from her son, acknowledging that each "new skill is so precious." We also may find joy when our child behaves like a typical child. I don't even remember exactly what he did, but I was delighted the first day my son acted like a typical teenager.

## Joys in the Child's Accomplishments

My younger son had so many health complications early in his life that we were told if he survived he would probably never experience the same accomplishments or successes as other children his age. This was not comforting news to hear as a parent. However, in many ways that bleak outlook helped us to enjoy each accomplishment along the way. Quite frankly, we have found joy not only in his constant growth and achievements but in the ways he has proved others wrong.

Many parents in this survey also found joy in the accomplishments and successes of their children, or as one set of parents put it, "accomplishing goals we thought were not possible." Children with ADHD often have difficulty finishing a task or a project before jumping to something new. Parents rejoice when a child with ADHD completes a task because of the extra work and effort required to accomplish ordinary tasks. Additional joys of parents include:

- "Seeing my child succeed, and get along with others, and when he shows love or empathy."

> Children with developmental challenges may not have the same accomplishments and successes of other children, but whatever they are able to achieve brings joy to their parents.

- "Watching them meet a challenge and succeed. Admiring their originality and spirit."
- "The first time my son wrote his name, the first time he read me a book in sign language, the first time he tied his shoes! When my ADHD kids are able to make friends and keep them."

Children with developmental challenges may not have the same accomplishments and successes of other children, but whatever they are able to achieve brings joy to their parents.

### Joys in the Child's Gifts or Qualities

Many parents find joy in the gifts or qualities of our children. One father finds joy in his son's "charm and character." A mother finds joy in the fact that her adult son is "loving, perceptive, and insightful." Other parents said,

- "I have a very creative, smart, funny kid."
- "[She is] so funny! So creative! So intelligent!"
- "He is an amazing athlete. His heart is huge! I love him in so many ways, just like I love all of my kids in so many ways."

Three different parents of children diagnosed with ASD mentioned the empathy of their child as one of the many traits that brings them joy as a parent.

- "My child is empathetic and does not judge the people in the world around him."
- "My son is empathetic, kind, and intelligent! He's a voracious reader, who remembers great details from what he reads."
- "Seeing the positive changes in this wonderful young man. I love watching him when he helps someone in need. I'm very proud of him. Seeing what an empathetic, loving young man he has become."

> Parents who see joy in our child's gifts or qualities see past the limitations of diagnosis.

Parents who see joy in our child's gifts or qualities see past the limitations of diagnosis. We do not allow the disorder to define the child. We allow and encourage the child to develop into their own person.

## *Joy Unique to ASD or ADHD Traits*

While many parents do not let our children be defined by ASD or ADHD, this does not stop us from finding joy in the traits that accompany the developmental challenges. I enjoy my son's attention to detail, a trait of autism. I appreciate that he notices when I get a haircut or a new outfit.

Children with ADHD are physically active but also have free and active minds in which these parents have found joy:

- "I am amazed by his thought process; he makes me laugh with his dry humor; his creativity amazes me."
- "My son is funny. His lack of impulse control at times allows some hilarious comments."
- "My ADHD son is so imaginative and so exuberant. It can be trying, but it's neat to watch the worlds he creates."

A few traits of people with ASD include repetitive routines, obsessive focus on a single object or topic, and ability to perceive patterns. One father stated his joy in his children's "unique perspectives, intelligence, detail, and patterns for reliability." A mother shared her joys:

> My daughter with ASD is so quirky and funny. She sees the world in such a different way from everyone else, and her delays make her act a little younger than her age so it's like getting to have a baby for a longer time than most parents. Every single time she plays nicely with another kid, I'm overjoyed; it's not a common, everyday occurrence. She also has this way of ordering her world in a way that can be so funny. Her "autism obsession" is monkeys, and she's decided that she is, in fact, a monkey rather than a little girl; since she clearly can't be a jungle animal in a family of humans, she's decided that I'm a giraffe and her brother is a lion (Daddy's species changes on a regular basis). Who says kids with ASD don't have imaginations?

Another trait of ASD is rigid adherence to rules, rituals, and facts. Therefore, some people with autism are not capable of lying. One parent shared the joys of her son, "He is very intelligent, he is terrible at lying. He is factual, unique, and his own person." Another mother appreciated her child's truth telling and ability to be intensely focused on the things he enjoys.

The senses of individuals with autism are often heightened. This often means that they are more responsive to sensory stimuli, like sights, sounds, and smells. One parent appreciated that her child has helped her "see things from a different point of view. We are much more in tune with our sensory environment." I have heard it said that children often raise the parents. In some ways that is true; all parents learn from our children. Parents of children with developmental challenges learn many things we wish we did not have to learn—medical terminology, how to find and work with developmental specialists—but we also learn to find joy in our child in ways we never thought we would.

## Sharing Joy

The observations I have shared in this chapter remind parents, family, friends, and members of faith communities that parents of children with developmental challenges do experience joy. It can be found in the child, in accomplishments, gifts, or qualities of the child, or in the unique traits of ASD or ADHD. Whatever gives us joy, we as parents definitely have joy down in our hearts for our children, and we want to share it.

Joy is contagious and is meant to be shared with others. My son has a gift for joy. When he is happy about something, it is a whole-body experience. He may clap or shout or rock or bounce or smile from ear to ear. It is difficult not to smile or experience joy by watching him. He is so fully present in the moment, enjoying the moment, that he shows me what pure joy is like. He doesn't hold back. I often feel my burdens as a parent, spouse, pastor, or professor take joy away from me. But when I see my son's joy, it is contagious and fills me with joy down in my heart. This joy reminds me of the

Parents of children with developmental challenges learn to find joy in our child in ways we never thought we would.

blessings I have—including my son—and gives me grace to see joy in life.

Family, friends, and members of faith communities, ask us what gives us joy as we parent our child. Listen. Rejoice with us as we celebrate the gift of our child and the joy we have down in our heart to stay.

## For Reflection and Discussion

1 What joys of the parents in this chapter surprised you? How did they surprise you?

2 (Parents) What are your joys as you parent your children?

3 (Parents) What joys of the parents in this chapter are similar to your own?

4 (Family and Friends) What joys do you experience with children with developmental challenges?

5 (Members of Faith Communities) How does your faith community celebrate children with developmental challenges?

# 3

# It Never Ends: A Cry of Challenge

It never ends—
    My child will always need support.
        As a teen
        As a young adult
        As an older adult

It never ends—
    My child will always need support
        As I grow older
        As I retire
        As I need more and more care

What happens when I come to an end?
    What happens to my child?
    My child will always need support.

—HHW

CHALLENGES ARE a given for any parent. Parents who have children with developmental challenges share some of the same difficulties as other parents, such as behavioral issues, homework struggles, or concerns about social interaction. However, behavioral issues may be intensified, homework struggles amplified, and social awkwardness enhanced compared to typical children. It takes more than finding the proper punishment to temper inappropriate behaviors. And it takes more than a busy social schedule to gain social skills. Sometimes it takes sleuthing to find out what is causing behaviors.

Repetitive coaching and teaching are required to help a child gain social skills.

I remember when my son was about seven years old, and we were going to the park for a picnic. I was making sandwiches in the kitchen when he asked, "Why a picnic?" I automatically responded, "Because it is a beautiful day outside." Then he asked again, "Why a picnic?" I said, "Because the sun is shining, and the weather is nice." He asked again, "Why a picnic?" I confess at this point I was starting to lose patience. I am not sure how I responded, but we went back and forth for a few more times. I was almost ready to offer the parental ultimate answer, "Because I said so!" But then I finally deduced the question he was actually asking. When I realized he was really asking, "What's a picnic?" I responded, "A picnic is when we eat our food outside." He walked away satisfied.

The challenges for parents of neurotypical children seem like they will never end. In reality, most children, including some developmentally challenged children, experience challenges— sometimes significant ones—for a while and then they ease or disappear altogether. For some parents of children with developmental challenges, the difficulties really will never end. Children with lifelong, complex needs will require support, sometimes longer than the parents are able to physically give support. All parents need courage and support to face the variety of challenges—for the long haul.

Behavioral issues, homework and school systems, others' misunderstandings, and relationships were some of the many challenges the parents in this survey mentioned when responding to the question "What are your challenges as you parent your child with Autism Spectrum Disorder, Attention-Deficit/Hyperactivity Disorder, and/or Fetal Alcohol Spectrum Disorder?"

The challenges for parents of neurotypical children seem like they will never end. For some parents of children with developmental challenges, the difficulties really will never end.

## Behavioral Issues

Often, parents will talk about a child's "behaviors" or "meltdowns." A parent knows when it is happening, and it is different from a child throwing a tantrum because they are stubborn and want their own way. When a child is in the middle of a "meltdown," no amount of reasoning, bribery, or anything else will work. The behavioral issues and meltdowns are often caused by the inability of the child to communicate or regulate their emotions or reactions, or both. What a "meltdown" looks like is different for each child, but it refers to a whole mind, body, and emotional reaction.

One mother described in detail the behavioral issues of her two young children:

> The biggest challenge by far is trying over and over again to teach impulse control to my ADHD son. He hits kids, and then he's sorry and cries, and then he hits them again. He hates that he can't control himself, and it frankly drives us more than a little crazy that we can't take him anywhere without worrying that we're going to see a bunch of kids sobbing and pointing at him because he hit them all. It's so hard to find the parenting balance; we don't want to be too hard on him because to some extent, he can't control it, but we also don't want to excuse bad behavior. For my daughter with ASD, a major challenge is that I'm her emotional bellwether. She has a very strong attachment to me, which in some ways is a wonderful thing. I know that some parents yearn for obvious signs of affection from their children with ASD and don't get it, and that's never been the case with my little bundle of hugs. It does mean, though, that if I'm even slightly upset about anything—whether or not it has to do with her—she bursts into tears. I have trouble disciplining her because it will lead to a half-hour tantrum, not because she's lost a privilege but because she's afraid I don't love her anymore. There are days I can't even discipline her brother without her having a tantrum because she's so upset that I'm raising my voice, even though it isn't directed at her! It can also be challenging to get the two of them to play together. He can be very rough and impulsive, and she likes everything in order; sometimes they play nicely, but part of me is always waiting for the yelling and tears to start.

What a "meltdown" looks like is different for each child, but it refers to a whole mind, body, and emotional reaction.

Note the complexities that the mother must keep in mind in working with each child. She understands her son's lack of impulse control but does not excuse his bad behavior. She must be aware that her daughter's responsiveness to her tone of voice can cause a reaction—even if it does not concern her daughter. Parents must tend to multiple issues at the same time, which can add stress to the exhausted parent's already busy life.

I have heard it said that children with autism need a longer runway—more time and space—to learn something. They need more time and space to transition from one thing to another. For example, in transitioning from the playground to leave to go home, we would give our children a notice that we were leaving in two minutes. It may or may not have been an actual two minutes, but it gave them time to transition. A longer runway is also needed to learn developmental skills. A mother of a teenager diagnosed with ASD and ADHD expressed difficulties with her daughter's "impulsivity, lack of self-control, poor thinking processes, and lack of improvement." It will take her daughter longer to learn these skills. She will need more reminders, more teaching, and more practice before her skills will improve. Parents can lose patience when progress is slow, especially when compared to neurotypical children.

The behavioral issues of children challenge parents to employ a variety of skills and responses. One mother of two adopted teenage sons diagnosed with ADHD talked about needing to have "a much bigger toolbox to handle behavior issues." She realizes that her sons' behavior issues require she add more skills and responses to her repertoire, which can be an ongoing process. A response that may help for one situation may not work for another or may only work one time. Another required skill this mother believes parents need in working with behavioral issues is "to be more self-differentiated and self-aware so that their [children's] needs can be met." Self-differentiated means the ability not to take the reactions of our children personally. This can be a difficult one for parents to learn. If we think our child's behavior is a personal attack on us, we react

Children with autism need a longer runway— more time and space— to learn something.

The behavioral issues of children challenge parents to employ a variety of skills and responses.

with emotion, which may not be helpful for us or the child. If we realize that our child's behavior is caused by something else, we look for what might be causing it.

Even with more tools, skills, and responses to work with our children and the behavioral issues, there are times when there is nothing a parent can do. One mother stated, "there is nothing that compares with 'meltdown mode.' And there is nothing to do except to give him space for him to express whatever caused the meltdown." It is never easy as a parent to watch our children go through something like that. Nonetheless we do. We continue to love our children and keep looking for ways to help. Another mother shared her challenges with parenting:

> The rules are different for my son. Sometimes he has outbursts. Sometimes he doesn't listen. Often, he argues with us when he doesn't agree with something. It can be exhausting. His ADHD makes it harder sometimes to parent my other children. If he can get away with this behavior, shouldn't my other kids, too? His behavior isn't always what I want modeled for my younger son. My son is an amazing athlete. But his ADHD paired with ODD [Oppositional Defiance Disorder] doesn't always work in his favor on the basketball court. His lack of impulse control and high passion means he argues with the ref's calls. He gets technical fouls more than anyone on his team, and we need to hold our heads high as parents in the stands. It's hard.

Parents require strength to face these behavior issues day after day, but it can take its toll. "Staying strong through bad days" is a challenge for any parent no matter the child. Strength is gained day by day in working with the child, getting help, learning skills, gaining response, and getting support. The behavioral issues of children with ASD, ADHD, and FASD differ from child to child. However, separating the child's behavior from the child themselves is central for parents and others to remember. The behavior may be unacceptable, but the child is always loved and accepted.

There is nothing that compares with "meltdown mode." And there is nothing to do except to give him space for him to express whatever caused the meltdown.

## Homework and School Systems

Often, school-age children with developmental challenges struggle with homework assignments. This can also lead to defiance and challenging behaviors. A mother of a preteen daughter, diagnosed with ADHD, shared how difficult it is "when she doesn't get her homework done before the meds wear off. Doing homework is pretty awful, the other day she told me she hated her brain and felt stupid." What do you do when your child says things like this? On the one hand, you feel the pain of your struggling child. On the other hand, you know that homework plays a role in education and that putting forth extra effort to learn is a valuable skill. The challenge for parents is to find a balance between excusing your child's behavior and holding expectations that work for your child. While addressing homework with her teenager, one mother said her son "argues constantly; he doesn't remember many things, lies, and doesn't follow basic instructions."

One mother of two adopted teen sons, both diagnosed with ADHD, detailed her challenges,

> My older son has ADHD, some OCD, and a Schizoid personality type. He cannot relate well socially to other people. He has few friends and has a very negative outlook on life. It is hard to keep a positive outlook with him. My younger son is very pleasant and original but doesn't want to do anything the conventional way with things that bore him such as chores and homework. He is smart but has a hard time finishing and handing in school assignments. His sense of time management is very different from ours, and it can be frustrating getting to places on time and finishing things in a timely manner.

Many parents experience challenges with the school system. The parent's struggle may be with the teachers, administration, or the process of getting help for their child at school. School systems may not offer the services or the type of support a particular child needs. A mother of a daughter with ASD and another daughter with ADHD wrote:

The challenge for parents is to find a balance between excusing your child's behavior and holding expectations that work for your child.

> I felt and still feel that I am in this alone, the school system is quite okay with letting them fall between the cracks, and if I say anything at all I am labeled [as a difficult or demanding parent] and told to back off and let my kid just be, but then the meltdowns increase, the emotional neediness gets worse.

When the school personnel are unresponsive or defensive, a parent can feel alone. Parents who experience difficulties with school systems may turn to homeschooling. But for children with extreme behavior problems, the parents do not have the stamina to teach and work with the behavior issues at home.

I served as a consultant to a faith community that had a special-needs parent support group. The parents of the support group wanted to educate the other members of the congregation about their children. In this faith community, a majority of the mothers homeschooled their children. Many of the parents in the support group had tried homeschooling, but due to their children's extreme behavioral issues, they were not able to do so. The other parents of the faith community told them the reason the children had behavioral issues was because they were not being homeschooled. The support-group parents felt judged and misunderstood by the other parents.

**Parents need to become advocates for our children.**

Tending to a child's educational needs adds extra stress and complexities to the task of raising a child with developmental challenges. Parents struggle with getting the child to complete homework while navigating the child's emotional and behavioral reactions to homework. At the same time, parents need to work with teachers and administrators of school systems to help arrange the services the child needs to learn and succeed. Sometimes children who need extra support in school slip through the cracks. Parents need to become advocates for our children. We cannot simply send our children to school and trust that the teachers and administrators will know how to do the best thing for our children. Parents of children with developmental challenges need to follow up and ask questions of teachers and administrators.

## Others' Misunderstanding

Other people's misunderstanding and disbelief are common challenges parents face. A mother of a young son with ADHD replied that she struggles with "not being able to get him the help he needs; other people not understanding his challenges, or even believing he actually has them." If people don't understand, that misunderstanding can be addressed with education. Educating people about ASD, ADHD, and FASD aids in understanding the issues or causes for a child's behavior and gives tips for working with the child. However, some people may never understand. When dealing with people who misunderstand, the parents of one teen diagnosed with ASD said, "[We] ignore others when they think we are 'pampering her' and her preferences." In some cases, ignoring others is necessary for your own well-being.

If people do not believe anything is wrong, that challenge is a lot more difficult to address. In my years as a pastor, I have met people who do not believe in God. In my younger years, I would try to convince and argue them into believing. In my later years, I have learned that I cannot argue anyone into believing. Faith is a gift. Now, I share my faith and my belief and live my life informed by faith, leaving the rest in God's hands. We can respond in the same way with those who don't believe anything is wrong with our children. We can state what we know, what it means, and what we have experienced and leave it there.

A mother of six children, each diagnosed with ASD or ADHD, commented on the many challenges of raising her children: "Biggest challenge is probably trying to help others understand my children aren't freaks or weird. They are a blessing." What are the blessings that other people cannot see? A blessing is something that gives life and joy (see chapter 2). Our children give us life and joy. Sometimes that can be easily identified and sometimes not. Their presence offers us something we may not experience without them. My son with autism has enriched and blessed my life—and the lives of other people—through his caring spirit and outlook on life.

Biggest challenge is probably trying to help others understand my children aren't freaks or weird. They are a blessing.

## Relationships

It is common for parents during these early years of parenting to put aside our own needs for friendships or relationships with others. The developmental challenges of our children can be so demanding that the parent has little time for self and friendships (for more on this, see chapter 6). This is a sacrifice many of us are willing to make. However, if we are feeling isolated and alone, it may be a sign we need to reach out to others.

Sometimes the relationship between parent and child is challenging. A mother pointed to the difficulty of "trying to tell him that we just want what is best for him, even if he can't see what that is." Another woman, who is caring for two adult men who have ASD and ADHD, shared that dealing with their daily outbursts and lack of self-control affects her relationship with them. She admitted that she struggles to "maintain a positive attitude and [offer them] forgiveness."

Sometimes the children have trouble maintaining relationships with others. Making and keeping friends is especially difficult for children with developmental challenges. A mother of two teens with ASD and ADHD said, "they do not have any friends or social interaction." Social interaction is part of growing up and learning how to engage with people. But it is also about companionship. Humans are social beings; we like to be with others and interact with them. As parents, we want our children to be part of a support system that includes people other than family members. It is scary for us to think about our children being alone and not having other people to call on for help or companionship.

## Facing the Challenges

Behavioral issues, homework, uncooperative school systems, others' misunderstandings, and awkward or nonexistent relationships are experienced by all parents. However, the unique characteristics of ASD, ADHD, and FASD add complexity for parents. What can help

> If we are feeling isolated and alone, it may be a sign we need to reach out to others.

parents face these challenges? Each of these challenges may require a different approach and each person is different. A good support system for the parent helps. That might include support groups, whether issue specific or for parenting in general.

Some schools offer education classes and opportunities to meet with other parents of children in special-education programs. My youngest son attended a preschool for children who were deaf or hard of hearing. The school sponsored a few events a year for families and students. I always appreciated connecting with other parents and children at these events. It helped me to share joys and challenges with others who understood my experience, and we could swap stories or resources with each other.

Parents need not face the challenging behaviors of our children alone. Certain agencies, like The Arc and the Pacer Center, specialize in education, advocacy, or support for people with ASD, ADHD, and/or FASD and their families. The Washburn Center for Children website offers resources for common family challenges.[1] Other supports for parents include therapists, child advocates, social workers, or behavioral specialists. Family and friends can support parents facing challenging times by listening and caring.

## For Reflection and Discussion

1 (Parents) What challenges do you experience with your children?

2 (Parents) What challenges in this chapter are similar to yours?

3 (Parents) What helps you to face the challenges you experience?

4 (Family and Friends) What are some of the challenges you see your family member or friend who has a child with developmental challenges experiencing?

5 (Members of Faith Communities) In what ways might your faith community offer support to parents who may experience challenges similar or different from those presented in this chapter?

# 4

## How Long? A Cry of Pain

How long, O Lord? Will you forget me forever?
  How long will you hide your face from me?
How long must I bear pain in my soul,
  and have sorrow in my heart all day long?
How long shall my enemy be exalted over me?

Consider and answer me, O Lord my God!
  Give light to my eyes, or I will sleep the sleep of death,
and my enemy will say, "I have prevailed";
  my foes will rejoice because I am shaken.

But I trusted in your steadfast love;
  my heart shall rejoice in your salvation.
I will sing to the Lord,
  because he has dealt bountifully with me.
—Psalm 13

THE WORDS of the psalmist have been my words more than once in my life. I especially turn to the first four questions: "How long, O Lord? Will you forget me forever? How long will you hide your face from me? How long must I bear pain in my soul, and have sorrow in my heart all day long?" I have spoken these words in quiet reverence, I have shouted them in loud defiance, and I have cried them in deep pain. Psalm 13 has been my expression when I have no words of my own I can utter to God. With deep pain, sometimes there are no words.

All parents experience pain while raising their children. Parents of children with developmental challenges experience deep pain when there is nothing we can do to prevent our children's struggles. One mother, responding to the survey question, shared her pain,

> My son has a disability. Nobody wants their child to have a disability. His ADHD interferes with his life. He will always have to deal with it in some way, and it is of no fault of his own. He doesn't want to be different. He doesn't want to argue with authority. He doesn't want to be out of control sometimes. And often times, he simply can't help it. His brain works differently. It causes me pain when people will make or post comments about kids with ADHD, saying they don't need medication, instead they just need to get outside and play more and get away from video games. No! My son is incredibly active. He plays outside all of the time. That might be helpful for him, but it certainly doesn't help all of his symptoms.

As a parent of a child with developmental challenges, I live with the pain that my son will never be on his own, that he will always struggle with life, and I cannot make it better. I have learned that speaking what causes me pain helps me release the pain. I have also noticed that many people are uncomfortable or don't know what to do when I give voice to that pain. Some want to talk me out of my pain, by finding ways that I could have it worse or by finding others who have it worse. But that has never helped my pain. It made me hurt for the people who have it worse, because I know that pain. Some people think expressing pain keeps one stuck in the pain and stuck in the emotions. I agree that can happen, but I believe offering parents who are suffering an opportunity to give voice to the pain helps the parent acknowledge it is there and—slowly, eventually—move through it.

## Sources of Pain

In the survey, I asked parents "What causes you pain as your raise your child with ASD, ADHD, or FASD?" As I attempted to pull together the variety of responses, so that they were not so unwieldy

I believe offering parents who are suffering an opportunity to give voice to the pain helps the parent acknowledge it is there and—slowly, eventually—move through it.

to read, I realized that pain is unwieldy. Pain resists organization and categorization. Yet, however unwieldy it is, I believe it is important for parents to express, as best we can, the reality of our pain, so that we may know how the experience is affecting us and to begin to let go of it.

## Bullying

According to PACER's National Bullying Prevention Center, more than one in five students will be bullied in each school year.[1] In addition, when a child has a disability, they are two to three more times more likely to be bullied.[2] As parents, we love our children with developmental challenges and see their gifts, but others may only see how the child is different.

A mother of six children with various developmental challenges expressed her pain at "seeing my children bullied or hurt because they realize they are different and people treat them different." Another mother of one daughter with ASD and another with ADHD said she feels pain "when I watch my kids get bullied and teased and the school says suck it up."

## Inadequate Social Skills

Another area of pain experienced by some parents of children with developmental challenges concerns social skills. Learning, understanding, and using social skills can be especially difficult for people with ASD and FASD, but often traits of ADHD also affect social skills. A father noted his pain for his young adult sons diagnosed with ASD and their "struggle to connect with others and not making friends." A mother said that she hurts "when [her daughter] doesn't understand things that other kids do."

One mother of a young adult daughter, diagnosed with ASD, shared her anguish at "watching her being left out. Watching her choose to do things on her own. Watching her try to be included in inappropriate ways. Watching her work so hard but not really 'get' why she's not getting anywhere." All parents want our children

> As parents, we love our children with developmental challenges and see their gifts, but others may only see how the child is different.

to have friends and to be part of a group instead of being left out. When the social skills are lacking, it is a greater challenge for the child and is difficult for the parent to watch. Sometimes the child is not aware of their lack of social skills. One mother said it was painful for her when her middle-school-age son admitted "he is 'too different'" from the other kids. She added, "when I see him excluded from groups of children, I hurt with him."

Other parents experience pain when their children get older and have not learned the skills they need. A mother of a young son with ADHD shared her sorrow in "watching my son try and fail, over and over again, to behave himself. He's upset that he can't do well, and I worry that he'll still be behaving this way in high school." A mother of a teenage daughter with ASD said what makes her heart ache is "that she struggles with things that I never had to. I can't always protect her. She needs to practice figuring out how to cope in healthy ways with the world."

Developing skills for navigating life in this world is tough enough without the added challenges of ASD, ADHD, or FASD. As parents, we want to protect our children, but that is not always possible. A mother of three adopted teenagers diagnosed with ADHD expressed her pain concerning this, "As they get older and I have to 'help' less, it hurts so much to watch them struggle, fail, and learn the hard way (or never learn those skills at all)." This is painful for a parent. A father of an adopted daughter in her mid-twenties, diagnosed with ADHD and FASD, expressed pain and exasperation at his daughter's "consistent failure at survival skills."

Sometimes what causes us pain as parents is not experienced the same way by our children, but that does not take away our pain. A mother of two teenage sons diagnosed with ASD and ADHD shared: "I think they would be lonely, but they say they aren't." It is difficult to know if the child means it or not. Children with ASD often do like being alone. In these cases, it bothers the parents more than the child.

As parents, we want to protect our children, but that is not always possible.

A parent's goal is to help their child learn skills to live on their own, but what if they never learn those skills? This an area of pain for some parents. One parent of an adult son with ASD simply shared, "I don't know if he's going to make it on his own." A mother of teen sons with ASD and ADHD shared the pain of "knowing they will require help their whole lives." Another mother of a toddler diagnosed with ASD shared her pain "knowing that it is a possibility that he will never talk."

### Guardianship

When a child turns eighteen years old, the parent is no longer legally able to make decisions for the child or get information about the child without the child's consent. Normally this is okay, but if a child is vulnerable already or does not have the verbal or intellectual skills to give assent, what is a parent to do?

A few years ago, I heard a story of a young woman who had developmental challenges. As she turned eighteen, she was on the borderline of needing extra support, but her parents had a good relationship with her, so they did not seek guardianship to help her make decisions. By the time she was twenty, she had found some "friends" who took advantage of her giving heart and her bank account. She gave them large amounts of money. The parents had no legal standing to protect her because she willingly gave them the money, whether or not it was in her best interests.

One of my greatest pains was realizing that my son would never learn the skills he needed to be fully independent. I want with all my heart for him to live on his own, to have a job with a living wage, pay bills, take care of his own needs, and make his own medical decisions. He may not be able to do these things without some type of support for the rest of his life.

As our son approached his eighteenth birthday, my husband and I realized the best way to help our son, as he entered legal adulthood, would be to have guardianship. But it was personally painful to me. I want to send him on his way, to be on his own in this world,

> I don't know if he's going to make it on his own.

but he is not ready. Even though his chronological age states that he is now an adult, he is vulnerable and not able to handle these responsibilities yet—if ever.

We started the process of gaining guardianship for our son a year in advance, receiving assistance from The Arc, talking with our son's case manager at school, and explaining the process to our son. He understood and was okay with guardianship. The day we were in court was a tough day for me. When it was our time to present our case to the judge, we sat on one side of the courtroom with our lawyer. Our son sat on the other side with his lawyer. I was called to the stand to witness that my son couldn't be an adult without assistance. This was gut wrenching for me. Also at court that day was another family with a son with autism who had more challenges than our son. As this young man was wandering the hall, flapping his hands and vocalizing without words, I heard his father explain to the lawyer, "I think he understands what's going to happen, but we will keep him out here until they are ready for him." What a painful but necessary decision some parents need to make.

Assuming guardianship of your child because they cannot attend to all the tasks of adulthood goes against everything a parent is supposed to do. But it is done in the best interests of the, now adult, child. Five years have passed since that day, and the pain is not as great as it was. Yet the fact remains, he will always need assistance of one type or the other. I am ready to move to the empty-nest-parent phase, but it is not yet time for him to make that move. We will have more conversations and make more decisions before we get to that point.

## *Pain Caused by Attitudes or Misunderstanding*

Some of the parents expressed that "other people's attitudes" about their child or "people not getting my kids" causes them pain. One mother of a middle-school-aged boy diagnosed with ADHD shared her anguish "watching others judge my kids and me and my husband in church and school. Seeing other teenagers have many friends and succeeding in school and activities." A mother of two adopted teenage sons with FASD said what causes her pain is when "people are not supportive and don't ask how they can help."

Pain caused by attitudes, misunderstandings, or not being supportive is not limited to people outside the family; it can be caused by family members themselves. It is not uncommon to have immediate family "not get my kids." This is distressing for the parent. However, what is even more distressing is when spouses are not supporting each other or working together to help the child.

One mother of a young adult son diagnosed with ASD and ADHD said what caused her pain is that "his father is still in denial that our child is not neurotypical."

When spouses disagree about parenting, it adds stress to the relationship. However, if one spouse is in denial there is anything wrong or different about the child, the parent who takes the lead in caring for the child experiences extra pain. This pain puts strain on the marriage. Even though studies suggest the divorce rate is the same for couples with children who have developmental challenges as the general population,[3] the stress and pain of having children with developmental challenges create more complications in marriage, as well as other family relationships.

### Depression and Anxiety

People who are diagnosed with ASD, ADHD, or FASD are more likely to experience depression or anxiety. This is caused by a variety of factors. For example, children with autism who like order and routine will experience anxiety at times of change or disruption to their schedule. Depression and anxiety on top of the child's other challenges adds to the pain of the parents as they watch their child struggle with one more thing. A father shared his pain "when [my son] says he doesn't have friends, when he says he isn't worth anything and doesn't want to live. He's been battling depression and anxiety the last two years." A mother of a teen daughter with ADHD agonizes "when my child is suffering because of the ADHD and/or anxiety. And I still wonder if it's my fault!!"

The stress and pain of having children with developmental challenges create more complications in marriage, as well as other family relationships.

Two parents confessed their own struggles with depression and anxiety. One mother raising her adopted son (now in his thirties), diagnosed with ADHD and FASD, admitted, "I ended up with anxiety attacks from the lack of sleep and the stress when he was an infant. Also, that he got into drugs and alcohol when he was a young teenager and damaged his brain. He now has very poor executive function." Another woman shared her pain, "I struggle with migraines as well as some depression and anxiety, and the stigma attached to seeking treatment for them."

With all the advances we have made as a society in the twenty-first century, I am sad we have not made much progress to lessen the stigma associated with depression and anxiety. Some people still see depression and anxiety as weakness or failure instead of a biological illness. I hope we can see people who experience depression or anxiety as people who are suffering and need help and support. Children who live with developmental challenges and their parents do not need more reasons to be seen as outcasts.

### Many and Varied

The pains experienced by these parents are many and varied. One mother could have spoken for many parents who have children with developmental challenges when she shared her pain as "wondering if I'm doing enough, if I'm doing the right things, and if we can help get him to healthy, successful adulthood."

Parents experience tension between wanting other people to understand the child's disability and wanting others to appropriately challenge their child. Another mother of a young adult diagnosed with ASD is troubled by "both people's lowered expectations of him and not giving him any slack for having a disability."

A couple of parents commented on pain caused by actions of their children. A woman parenting two adult males diagnosed with ASD and ADHD shared her pain as "not being able to help [them] and [their] physical aggression." A mother of a teenage son with ADHD said, "It doesn't seem like he likes or loves me many days; [that he

> Parents experience tension between wanting other people to understand the child's disability and wanting others to appropriately challenge their child.

is] ungrateful; but having ADD myself . . . I know his struggles are real."

Others expressed discouragement in watching their child struggle. One mother mentioned her sorrow over her daughter "not having the same milestones as kids [her] same age." A grandmother noted her anguish for her grandson diagnosed with ASD "not having the same teenage experiences as regular school." While a mother of a son and daughter with ADHD shared her heartache "seeing the pain they feel when they are rejected by peers, when they can't accomplish something they are working toward."

One mother grieved her child's complex health issues:

> Not only does [my daughter] have ADHD and ASD, but she also has Huntington's Disease, which is much worse yet. All skills will deteriorate, and she will die. Knowing she will lose the ability to talk, walk, eat. . . . That she will never grow up. That she will be less and less normal.

**Whatever pains parents experience, it still does not negate the love we have for our children.**

The pains of parents of children with developmental challenges are many and varied. It includes the reality that our children are more likely to experience bullying, struggle in social relationships, or may never be able to live on their own; that others—even close family members—will never understand; or that other complications create less than ideal situations. Whatever pains parents experience, it still does not negate the love we have for our children. The reality is that pain is part of the experience of parenting and at times needs to be expressed and acknowledged by the parents.

## A Response to Pain

It is difficult to sit with someone and listen to their pain without wanting to solve it for them. The Hebrew Scriptures contains the long and complicated story of Job, who experiences many losses. It begins with God bragging to Satan about Job's devotion and faithfulness (Job 1:8), but Satan says Job is faithful because God is protecting him from hardship (Job 1:9–11). In a matter of a few verses, Job loses his livestock and his servants (Job 1:14–17) and then his children (Job 1:18–19). Soon, he develops terrible sores all over his body (Job 2:7–8), and his wife turns against him (Job 2:9). Job's friends come to "console and comfort" him. They sit with him in silence for seven days, "for they saw that his suffering was very great" (Job 2:11–13).

Then Job speaks. Out of misery and deep pain he despairs of his birth (Job 3:1–26). What follows is chapter after chapter of Job's friends finding reasons for his pain. Every argument they present, Job counters. Finally, in the end, God answers Job (Job 38:1–40:2, 40:6–41:34). God doesn't give reasons for Job's suffering, instead God gives a nature lesson, but God finally does respond. For Job, what is important is not that he know the reasons for his suffering but that God hears Job's cries and struggles and God speaks to him.

It is tricky to sit with others in their pain. Job's friends lasted only a few days before they were compelled to speak. Unfortunately, they concluded the most useful thing they could do was to convince Job that he must have done something to deserve what was happening to him. Job's friends could have cared for Job by continuing to listen to him share his pain. They could have cared for Job by bringing food or getting salve for his sores. Or they could have said they were sorry he was going through this suffering and they wished they could take it away. Today, many people act just as Job's friends did, and it is still not a supportive response to life's difficulties.

I remember after my oldest son was born four months early, people struggled to find words to say to me. One friend who was pregnant, due around the time my son was supposed to be born, said, "At least you know the gender of your baby." I did not find that helpful. However, another friend, the first time she saw me after my son was born, gave me a hug and said, "I don't know what to say." This was the most helpful thing anyone said to me during that time, because I didn't really know what to say either. I was able to express my pain and anguish with her while she sat with me and listened.

## For Reflection and Discussion

1 What thoughts or feelings came to you as you read this chapter?

2 (Parents) What causes you pain as you parent your child with developmental challenges?

3 (Parents) Is it helpful for you express your pain? If so, how is it helpful?

4 (Family or Friends) You may not be able to take away your friend or family member's pain, but how may you offer them support?

5 (Members of Faith Communities) Often faith communities do not allow people to express pain, thinking they are not trusting God if they do. What stories or verses in Scripture allow expressing pain to God as a cry of faith?

# 5

## Conviction of Things Not Seen:
## A Cry of Faith

"Faith is the assurance of things hoped for, the conviction of things
    not seen," the Bible says.
        Faith sounds pretty shaky to me,
            "*assurance* of things *hoped for*"?
            "*conviction* of things *not seen*"?
    Is faith shaky?
    I guess it can feel that way
        Tentative—not assured
        Timid—not convincing
    Is faith strength?
        Assurance—in something outside of yourself
        Assurance—that things are not in your control
        Conviction—God is present
        Conviction—God will work things out
    I float between feeling
        tentative and assured
        timid and convicted.
    Yet as a person of faith
        I believe I cannot do this on my own,
        I need God's grace and Jesus's love
        I need others
            to keep the faith
            to pray
            to hope
                for me when I struggle.

Faith is
> the assurance of things hoped for
> the conviction of things not seen.

—HHW

FAITH IS a relationship with God. A relationship involves give and take, effort and investment by both parties.

I rely on my faith to help me face everyday life as well as life with my son with developmental challenges. My relationship with God has grown and developed through reading and studying Scripture, through my involvement in the Christian (Lutheran) tradition, and through my life experience. I believe in a God who comes to us in Jesus Christ, who freely chooses death and the grave and is raised by God, so that even death will not have the last word. Because of Jesus's life, death, suffering, and resurrection, God knows what it is like to be human, to suffer, and to experience pain. This God enters my life through the Holy Spirit so that I am not alone in my joy or pain or suffering or life's challenges. God gives me hope and encouragement, even when the way is tough and the pain is great.

Faith is a relationship with God, and sometimes relationships are complicated. I have been angry at God at certain times in my life, especially when our youngest son, born prematurely, was near death for the first six weeks of his life. Because of my comfort level in my relationship with God, I can express my anger. Some people are not comfortable being angry at God. I believe if God cannot handle my anger, God has no business being God. God wants to have a relationship with us, which means that we can share everything that is going on within us as we would share with our friends. The lament psalms have taught me that it is even okay to complain to God.

People come to faith and experience their relationship with God in different ways. Yet, God is always working in and through people and reaching out to everyone. One's faith can be supported and

Faith is a relationship with God, and sometimes relationships are complicated.

nourished through prayer, worship, Scripture, music, art, community, Bible studies, tradition, or sacraments. In the survey, I asked, "What faith resources, if any, have you found helpful?" The responses of the parents included spiritual practices both of their personal faith and of the faith community to which they belong.

## Personal Faith

Many parents have a relationship with God, or a higher power, and find it helpful while raising a child with developmental challenges. Prayer is the most common spiritual practice people turn to. Prayer is speaking and listening to God. Whether or not the prayers are identifiably answered, knowing God has listened can offer strength and encouragement. In the quiet space of prayer, a person may receive clarity or direction. It may be that the person suddenly gets an idea or feels better without really knowing how or why. In her survey, one mom wrote, "without prayer I wouldn't make it. . . . I pray a lot." Another mother who adopted five children, each with developmental challenges, responded, "Faith? Oh, my goodness, without faith and prayer I wouldn't make it! It wouldn't be possible for me to parent these kiddos." In prayer, both of these parents find help, support, direction, and encouragement.

Some parents answered, "God is in control." Knowing God is in control offers comfort in trusting that God will take care of us even in difficult times. The parents of an adoptive son, diagnosed with ADHD and FASD (now in his thirties), stated, "We believe that God brought him to us. We feel bad that we were not able to more adequately meet his needs, but I suspect that we provided him with the best option available."

These parents offer both a lament and a statement of faith. Faith can be like that; one can complain and rejoice in the same breath. Complaint can be as much of a statement of faith as praise is. The lament psalms in the Hebrew Scriptures often begin with complaint and move to praise; both are a statement of faith in God.

One can complain and rejoice in the same breath. Complaint can be as much of a statement of faith as praise is.

Conversations with family or friends may be important for a parent's personal faith. One mother said that she and her husband "have had many in-depth conversations regarding religion, faith, community, and stewardship throughout the years" with family, friends, and members of their faith communities. Another mother shared that for her as a parent and a person of faith, "honest conversations with my colleagues and friends make a huge difference."

Online resources and social media provided strength and support for some parents in their relationship with God. One mother mentioned a specific faith-based Facebook group for people "who are parenting special-needs children that has been supportive" of her and her faith. Other parents found helpful Facebook groups for parents in similar situations. Some of these were faith-based, others not. Support groups do not necessarily have to be faith-based in order to strengthen and nurture one's relationship with God.

Personal faith may also be encouraged and strengthened through reading. One woman found certain authors, such as C. S. Lewis and Madeleine L'Engle, helpful to her. Sometimes stories can speak in ways that inspire and encourage one's relationship with God. Other parents mentioned reading Scripture. Reading Scripture can be as mysterious as prayer. You may or may not be able to describe exactly how your faith is nurtured and your relationship with God strengthened. There have been times when I have felt God speaking directly to me through Scripture. One mother specifically said Romans 8 was helpful and encouraging for her personal faith.

This powerful chapter includes verses I have found helpful in my personal life and in parenting a child with developmental challenges. Shortly after our younger son was born, my bishop came to visit with us at the hospital. His presence and care showed us God's love and grace. The Scripture he chose to read was Romans 8:18, "I consider that the sufferings of this present time are not worth comparing with the glory about to be revealed to us." We were experiencing deep pain and suffering at that time; our son was so sick we were not sure he was going to make it. I remember saying

> Support groups do not necessarily have to be faith-based in order to strengthen and nurture one's relationship with God.

> Personal faith may also be encouraged and strengthened through reading.

to the bishop, somewhat sarcastically, "That had better be some glory!" Fortunately, the bishop kept reading:

> The Spirit helps us in our weakness; for we do not know how to pray as we ought, but that very Spirit intercedes with sighs too deep for words. And God, who searches the heart, knows what is the mind of the Spirit, because the Spirit intercedes for the saints according to the will of God. (Rom 8:26–27)

This was helpful. I didn't know how to pray during this time—I was crying and sighing a lot. Hearing that the Spirit was praying for me comforted and encouraged me during this time of suffering. Then the bishop closed with this passage from Romans 8:

> Who will separate us from the love of Christ? Will hardship, or distress, or persecution, or famine, or nakedness, or peril, or sword? . . . No, in all these things we are more than conquerors through him who loved us. For I am convinced that neither death, nor life, nor angels, nor rulers, nor things present, nor things to come, nor powers, nor height, nor depth, nor anything else in all creation, will be able to separate us from the love of God in Christ Jesus our Lord. (Rom 8:35–39)

Nothing will separate us from the love of God. Not this suffering. Not this pain. Not this near-death experience. We are still held by God's love. Often during that long hospitalization, those words would come to mind and carry us through the difficult days.

## Faith Communities

Faith communities may play an important role in one's faith journey. Parents of children with developmental challenges often desire to be part of a faith community that will nurture their and their child's relationships with God.

Some parents have had positive experiences in their faith community. Staff and members of the community have worked to include the parents and children in all aspects of their life together.

Nothing will separate us from the love of God. Not this suffering. Not this pain. Not this near-death experience. We are still held by God's love.

One mother stated, "My church community is awesome. Our youth group was very accepting and accommodating as [my son] came in as a freshman." This occurred even though her family had just moved to the area and the leaders and youth-group members did not know her son. Another mother is a member of a faith community with a support group for parents of children with special needs. The group meets monthly "to present our prayer requests to each other and to 'check in' about all that has happened since the last meeting." The group has helped her endure some challenging times with her son and nurtured her relationship with God.

Unfortunately, some parents experienced faith communities not supportive of them or their children with developmental challenges. One father of an adopted daughter with ADHD and FAS shared, "We seem to have been abandoned by faith community." Another parent said "church leaders want kids to fit in a mold. They have no tolerance for anyone who is different."

Faith communities are imperfect, but at their best they are a place where parents and children with developmental challenges are supported and encouraged in their relationship with God. Members of faith communities may think they need an expansive program or to be experts in child development to engage with children with developmental disabilities and their families. However, all that is needed is an ability to listen and care for each person as a child of God.

Life in a faith community is central to my family. My children were raised going to worship every Sunday. When he was younger, it was challenging for my ASD son to be still and quiet in worship, except when it came time for Holy Communion. As soon as the pastor lifted the bread in Communion liturgy, my son stopped wiggling and watched. He was intently focused on this part of the worship service. He sang and spoke the responses with the congregation. He reverently walked forward to receive Communion. After returning to his seat, he would lift his bangs with his right hand and use his

Faith communities are imperfect, but at their best they are a place where parents and children with developmental challenges are supported and encouraged in their relationship with God.

left forefinger to make the sign of the cross on his forehead. Then he was noisy and wiggly until the end of the worship service. I don't know what was going on inside of him, but it was a holy moment for me. It reminded me that my son is a child of God; he and God are in relationship. Even though my son is active in worship, God is active, too.

## For Reflection and Discussion

1  What faith resources do you find helpful in your life?

2  Is being part of a faith community important to you? Why or why not?

3  (Parents) Is it important to raise your child in a faith community? Why or why not?

4  (Members of Faith Communities) What do you think are the important aspects of your faith community in which all people should be able to participate?

# 6

## Grace for the Day: Wisdom to Care for Self

Dear God, give me the grace to find small ways to be renewed, refreshed, and strengthened this day.

—HHW

WHEN OUR youngest son came home for the first time, after spending his first five months in the hospital, he was on seventeen doses of medication and an every-three-hour feeding schedule around the clock—seven, ten, one, and four o'clock. That meant my husband and I had to get up twice in the middle of the night to feed him. One of us would take the one o'clock in the morning feeding and the other one the four o'clock feeding. Our son had difficulty swallowing, so it took him about twenty minutes to drink two ounces of formula. In addition, he was crying and irritable much of the day. Those were tough times. His feeding issues and daytime irritability persisted for many months.

At the time, we lived in a rural area far away from friends and family members. I was working full time as a parish pastor, and my husband was a stay-at-home dad. When I came home, he was ready for a break, so I took over. But sometimes after a busy or demanding day of work, I was a tired and irritable. Due to our son's complications, my husband and I did not trust anybody to babysit unless they had received training to take care of him. We were stressed from lack of sleep and our son's feeding issues and daytime fussiness, not to mention we also had a two-and-a-half-year-old son to tend to at the same time. As a parent you make sacrifices to care for your children, but it was taking a toll on us. A couple of months after our son came home from the hospital, I was talking to the organist at the congregation I was serving as pastor. I told her of my son's complications and my sleep deprivation. The organist was also a nurse who worked the night shift at a local hospital. She offered to take care of our son one night every other week so that we could sleep through the night. Two full nights of sleep per month sounded amazing at that time, and we took her up on her offer. That little break did wonders to help us get through those challenging months.

Self-care is important for one's emotional, physical, and spiritual health. It is an over-simplification to say, "When mom and dad are happy, everyone in the family is happy," but it is not too far from the truth. As parents find ways to care for ourselves and take a break from the stresses of parenting, we will be better parents for our children. Parenting takes physical and emotional energy. You need to think about how to respond to behaviors or words your child says. You adjust your responses based on the age of your child and their abilities. You balance whether or not it is good for your child to have everything they want. You need to know when to do things for your child and when to encourage them to do it themselves. If you have had a tough day or are tired or stressed and your child is crying or asking you over and over again for something you have already declined, you may not respond in the best way.

Parents who have children with developmental challenges simultaneously experience increased stress and decreased opportunities to get a break. The complex needs of the child require a higher level of care and responsibility, so dropping the child off with the grandparents or a teenage babysitter is not always an option.

Since I know self-care is important for parents, I asked, "What do you do to take care of yourself?" Every parent who responded to

> Self-care is important for one's emotional, physical, and spiritual health.

this survey struggles with self-care because caring for their children with developmental challenges is their first priority.

A parent of two daughters (one diagnosed with ASD, the other ADHD), who is also a pastor, shared her dilemma: "I find it very difficult [to care for myself], because there is no one to watch the kids with their difficulties, and as a pastor, professional boundaries make it hard to ask much of any one." Another mother of a large family with biological and adopted children wrote that self-care

> is something I struggle with greatly, and I need to find a way to tend to me more often. I'm not good at taking time for myself until I'm just worn out, but a good cup of coffee and a few minutes of quiet can go a long way. I know as I age, I need to take more time for me, and I'm working on this, but with twelve kids and most with some form of special need, finding that is hard!

Parents neglect self-care for various reasons, including lack of time, energy, or resources. Some parents find themselves in the "sandwich generation," caring for children and aging parents at the same time. One mother, married to a pastor, shared the complexity of circumstances that affect her self-care:

> For years I didn't have time to take care of myself. I had two active boys, a husband who worked all the time, and elderly parents and parents-in-law who needed my attention. My kids don't need as much supervision as they have in the past. My husband has changed churches, and two of our four parents have died. I have tried to get more medical attention for depression and chiropractic care, but that's about it.

This mother also lives in a rural area with limited resources for self-care, such as counseling, respite services, or support groups for parents of children with developmental challenges. Many parents in this survey reported that they did very little to nothing to care for themselves. One father said, "I don't [care for myself]. I have too much other stuff to take care of." This experience is all too common.

## Little Things That Make a Difference

Some parents find that little things make a difference when life gets stressful. For example, a mother of four sons, one diagnosed with ADHD, considered taking walks and eating chocolate as self-care. A grandmother, raising her teenage grandson diagnosed with ASD, said she gets an occasional massage. A mother of a teenage son with ASD and ADHD said, "I knit or crochet nearly every evening; that is my relaxation activity."

Parents may not need to take a weekend retreat or a lengthy vacation without children to be refreshed and renewed. Little things like gardening, bicycling, or laughing may be ways of caring for oneself. Some parents found talking to their own parents or spending time alone or with their spouse to be self-care activities. Other activities may include making crafts, baking, exercising, reading, or going for drives alone in the country.

I found strength for my journey in little things like walks, visiting the family farm, and working outside in the yard or garden. My husband and I did not take much time away from our children, especially when they were younger and had complex needs. But we would take a yearly family vacation, sometimes going camping, which was good self-care. Even though car travel and camping can be stressful, we learned ways to make it successful for us and our children. We would take frequent breaks and travel only a few hours a day on long car trips. These family vacations were important for our self-care, and we also created many family memories during these trips.

Parents find creative ways to care for themselves and their children. One mother of a teenage son diagnosed with ADHD gives herself "time outs." She described it this way: "Mommy 'time outs' are good for me and teach the child that mom can only take so much, but she still loves you. Everyone needs time alone to cool down and think about what they have done." Another mother said, "I try to spend some time before the family wakes up reading my devotions.

> Little things like gardening, bicycling, or laughing may be ways of caring for oneself.

I go on my church's annual women's retreat." She also said, "I don't feel bad for watching TV or just being lazy when I'm not working and the kids are at school." Sometimes as parents we can give ourselves permission to be unproductive.

## Receiving Counseling

The cares and burdens of parents of children with developmental disabilities sometimes are more than one can handle on one's own. Many parents include counseling on their list of self-care activities.

Working with a counselor to develop skills and strategies is good self-care. A mother of a toddler diagnosed with ASD mentioned, "I take naps with my son whenever possible. I don't stress the small stuff and pick my battles. I also just take one day and one therapy session at a time." A counselor can help us decide what is important and what is not. The practice of taking one day at a time may be easier for some parents than others. A counselor can aid in learning to do that.

Family counseling may be helpful for some parents and children with developmental challenges, as well as the neurotypical siblings. The value of family counseling is that all the members of the family can work together on issues, listen to one another, and help each other. Sometimes when a parent focuses on the child with developmental challenges, the other children or spouse feels left out.

## Adjusting Attitudes

Adjusting attitudes and expectations may be a form of self-care. One father, who has a son with ASD, outlined his self-care routine as "volunteering, spending time with friends and family, as well as lowering expectations." Lowering expectations is not about letting the child get away with behaviors that are not acceptable. Nor does it mean a parent has given up on the child. It is about realizing that our expectations may be placing undue stress on ourselves, as well as our child.

Adjusting attitudes and expectations may be a form of self-care.

My husband and I have had to adjust our attitudes and expectations while raising our son. We have kept some expectations and adjusted others. For example, attending weekly worship was an expectation, but we had to adjust our thinking about what that looked like. Since I was leading worship every Sunday when our children were young, it was up to my husband to guide them through a worship service. He would have the boys follow the motions of worship. He would move his finger on the hymnbook page under the words of the liturgy or the hymns so that they could learn how to follow along.

But all this was more difficult for our son with autism, who was moving and singing much of the time. We couldn't stop him from moving or singing, but we could limit those actions to a better time. The rules of worship became: "Stand when we stand. Sit when we sit. Sing when we sing." The reality was that he would wander into the aisles when the congregation stood. Sometimes he would shout when the congregation sang. And the best we could hope for was wiggling a little less noisily when the congregation sat. We adjusted our expectations many times over the years, and sometimes during the same worship service. But changing our expectations became a way to care for ourselves—by not adding to our stress during these situations and finding ways for our son to participate in worship the best that he could at the time without being disruptive to the rest of the congregation.

## Educating Ourselves

Learning more about developmental challenges may also be a self-care skill. A mother of an adopted young adult son and a teenage son said she "reads a lot about ADHD, teenage brains, and defiant kids." Some parents read personal stories by people who have autism or ADHD. Educating oneself, as best as one can, about the child's developmental challenges, a parent gains confidence and skills to help the child.

Talking to and learning from other parents of children with similar challenges is an act of self-care. Another mother of a young

> Learning more about developmental challenges may also be a self-care skill.

daughter with ADHD said, "having mom friends with kids who also have anxiety or ADHD issues is a good thing." It is good for one's self-care to share with others who have similar experiences. During the many months my children spent in the NICU, I attended a weekly support group for mothers whose babies were in the NICU. The social worker guided us as we shared our stories, but she also educated us on the NICU experience. Both support and education were important to me and the other mothers in the group as we sought to care for our babies and ourselves during a time of great stress.

## Nurturing Friendships

Many of the parents in this survey mentioned talking or spending time with friends as part of a self-care plan. Whether or not the friends have children with developmental challenges, friends are important. Exactly what they talk about with their friends or how they spend time with friends may not be important. Friends can offer care, love, and support, often by simply showing up and listening. Many parents feel shame concerning their child's diagnosis. One mother realized the freeing power of speaking honestly with friends about what is going on with her son. "I talk honestly about my son's diagnosis [ADHD] rather than hide it with shame." Friends listening without judging dispels the power of shame.

Friends come and go throughout one's life. Each friend enriches our life in different ways, whether they are friends for a long time or a short time. Over the years, I have noticed some friendships drift apart because my friends were not able to understand what I was going through with my son. At the same time, I have been surprised by some strong, lasting friendships that have developed over the years.

If you are a parent of a child with developmental challenges, good self-care will include finding ways to keep the friendships you already have and to nurture new ones. Friends can offer support, encouragement, or distraction during this journey. Tending to

Friends can offer care, love, and support, often by simply showing up and listening.

friendships can be challenging. At times in my life, I have done this more successfully than others. You may need to be creative in the way you spend time with friends. One stay-at-home mother of two young children (daughter with ASD and son with ADHD) has "weekly Skype dates with friends to make sure that I'm talking to adults."

If you are a friend of someone caring for a child with developmental challenges, find ways to reach out to your friend. Sometimes a phone call or a walk with them is all they need. Other times, a distraction or time to laugh or play might be needed. Types of friendships and ways friends support each other vary, but central to all friendships is caring for each other.

There is no one way to care for self. Self-care usually consists of a variety of activities, strategies, even attitudes. If you are a parent of a child with developmental challenges and find yourself stressed by things that didn't bother you before, it may be a sign you need to tend to yourself. If you are a friend or family member of someone with a child with developmental challenges, support and encourage them to find ways to care for themselves. Parents are not at our best when we are running ourselves into the ground. It is important to care for ourselves as we care for our children.

## For Reflection and Discussion

1  What do you do to care for yourself?

2  What thoughts or feelings came to you as you read this chapter?

3  (Parents) If you think you do not do enough to care for yourself, how might you expand your self-care plan?

4  (Family and Friends) How might you help your friend or family member get self-care time?

5  (Members of Faith Communities) How might your faith community assist parents of children with developmental challenges to care for themselves?

# 7

# Listen Up! Wisdom to Share

Listen up!
If one more person tells me what I should do
      I will scream!
         Don't should me!
            Come alongside.
            Offer to help.
            Do something
         Instead of making my burden heavier.
            If one more person . . .

Maybe if my stress wasn't so great
    I would respond better to these "friendly" suggestions.
        You should just relax, it's not a big deal.
        You should call the teacher.
        You should take him to a new specialist.
        You should change her diet.

Hey! Look at it from my point of view,
    I have responsibilities
        for myself
        for my child
        for my family
        for my future
        for my child's future

Today I can't take on any more responsibility.
    If only one person, would
        Hear my cry.

Listen to my pain.
Share my joy.
Hold on to hope when I cannot.
Pray when I cannot pray.
Care for the frazzled part of me.

Listen up!
If one person would,
   Then the "shoulds"
      Would end their shame.

—HHW


"IF YOU were to write an instruction book for family, friends, or faith communities about parenting a child with Autism Spectrum Disorder, Attention-Deficit/Hyperactivity Disorder, and/or Fetal Alcohol Spectrum Disorder, what would you include? What do you want them to know? What are ways they might help you?"

Both the quality and the quantity of parents' responses to this survey question amazed me. They had a lot of advice to share. Some of the parents who wrote brief responses to the previous questions wrote lengthy responses to this question. Three distinct target audiences emerged from the responses. The parents offered wisdom to other parents, family members and friends, and faith communities. What follows is their wisdom born out of their personal experience.

## Life Is Like a Box of Chocolates: Wisdom for Parents

One mother offered this wisdom, "Life is hard; it's like a box of chocolates. Every day is different, and you never know what you're going to get." The wisdom offered by these parents for other parents is also like a box of chocolates, ranging from general to specific, from what to do for yourself to what to offer your child.

One parent of two adult males diagnosed with ASD and ADHD offered this general advice from her experience, "No matter the disability, maintaining structure, consistency, and enforcing rules early on in life will help them grow and be independent. Parents seem to baby their children, only causing them to be less independent and a lot more reliant." A grandmother offered this, "Be accepting of your child's differences and love them twice as much. Give them encouragement when they're not sure of a certain situation."

### Encouragement for Parents

A mother offered this encouragement for other parents, "It's a hard road, but if you find the right people, it makes the journey easier." Often parents need encouragement to "hang in there," to keep at it through the tough times. One father said, "It's hard . . . it's sad and happy and loud and quiet—all at the same time—but worth it." Even with the stress of their children's developmental challenges, it is important to state that for every parent in this study, it has been worth it.

One mother of a young daughter diagnosed with ADHD shared her wisdom:

"Patience is the thing you need the most of and the thing that seems to be in shortest supply. Every kid is different. Definitely ask for help! Blaming yourself is never useful. Support groups (formal or informal) are so helpful for me." A mother of an adopted son who lives with ADHD and FASD encouraged parents to

> talk to supportive friends or family members and have hobbies or activities you enjoy. If there is a support group available, go to it. . . . Be grateful there is more help available now than there was thirty years ago.

She is wise to point out that there is more help available today, and there will likely be even more help tomorrow. The idea of looking with gratitude at what is available, rather than ingratitude for what is not, is commendable. It is easy to find the flaws in the systems around diagnosis and care and understanding, because there are so many. But what would it be like for us as parents, in the midst of

It's a hard road, but if you find the right people, it makes the journey easier.

Definitely ask for help!

tough days, to find one thing to be thankful for? It might encourage us and help us to "hang in there."

### Advocate for Children

The wisdom of these parents included advocating for children. One mother said, "Be your child's advocate but teach them to recognize their situation as an explanation for their behavior, not an excuse. Love, love, love, love, no matter how many times you mess up." It is inevitable you will mess up as a parent. You will make mistakes or handle a situation inaptly. Continuing to love your child and yourself through it all is important.

Another mother of a young adult diagnosed with autism replied, "School was always a struggle [for my son], so I learned and became an advocate [for him]. There are little to no resources for parents of adult [children with developmental disabilities]." The role of advocate may change as the child ages, but in many cases the need to keep advocating for the child continues. There is a lack of information and resources for young adults and adults with developmental challenges. Once the school years are over, services or programs for them are more challenging to find.

Yet another mother encouraged persistence in advocacy: "Advocate for your child at school, and then follow up, and then follow up again! Find the things that work for your child and your family. Don't worry about what anyone else thinks is 'normal.' Just do what you need to do to set your child up for success."

### Concerning Autism Spectrum Disorders

Parents of children with Autism Spectrum Disorders addressed other parents of children with ASD. Parents of a preschool-age son said for them it is important "knowing that we are not alone in the struggle to raise a child with ASD." If they were to write an instruction book about ASD, they would like people to know about "less common markers and behaviors, early intervention, and our rights like IEP's

> Love, love, love, love, no matter how many times you mess up.

> Don't worry about what anyone else thinks is "normal." Just do what you need to do to set your child up for success.

and so on . . . also different places to go for help, both private and government."

A mother of a preschool-age daughter offered this wisdom for parents of children with ASD:

> I'd encourage them to get as much help as possible as soon as possible. It really does make a difference. My daughter has spent the past year in a special-needs school and received speech and occupational therapy on the side; she went from barely putting together three-word sentences to "I'm looking at the birds flying in the sky" after just a week at her special-needs school. It makes a huge difference, and that means there's hope!

Early identification and education for children with autism is effective for both children and parents. Teachers in early childhood education programs with autism training have expertise to engage with children and find ways for them to succeed. My son had better success in school when he switched from a regular special-education teacher to a teacher who specialized in autism. My son's teachers also helped *us* understand him, how autism affected him, and what we could do to help him.

One father of two young adult sons diagnosed with autism offered many pieces of wisdom. He encouraged parents to

> be aware of sensory issues such as volume of music and over stimulation, have a place to retreat and don't force social situations. Get them involved in volunteering together so they can be around others with structure for interaction. Help them find words, explain everything and what is an appropriate response. [Have] a lot of patience. Enjoy them for who they are and their interests.

Enjoy your child. Simple words of wisdom from which all parents can benefit.

Enjoy your child.

### *Concerning Attention-Deficit/Hyperactivity Disorder*

A mother of a teenage son diagnosed with Attention-Deficit/ Hyperactivity Disorder shared, "Kids with ADHD are not bad kids; it's a chemical imbalance, more discipline doesn't fix the problem; watch for eating disorders; hugs help a lot; be prepared to be heavily involved in your child's education." Another mother had this wisdom for parents:

> First of all, for ADHD, I'd tell parents to ignore the haters and horror stories. If you feel in your gut that your kid has more trouble controlling himself than his peers, there might be something wrong. And medication isn't scary and won't turn your kid into a zombie; if it has bad side effects, there are other types you can try. I was afraid to even tell some of my friends that we'd started medication for our son because they'd been acting as though medication were pure poison.

Reactions, side-effects, and effects of medication or therapies differ from one child to another. No one knows your child better than you do. Hold on to that when you are listening to others. Trust you own gut instinct.

One father said:

> Listen to your gut, but also listen to the advice of veteran teachers. Don't be afraid to put your kid on medication. It ended up being a very good decision for my son. It helped him focus in school. He wasn't reading on grade level at the time—first grade. He pretty much caught up with his classmates by second grade. He's now a junior and has had above a 4.0 average all year.

A mother of a middle-school-age son advised:

No one knows your child better than you do. Hold on to that when you are listening to others.

As far as ADHD is concerned, it isn't a bad thing! These kids are creative and energetic. It can be exhausting, especially when they are young, but the ideas they come up with and the focus they have when they are excited about something is amazing! Know that your kids will probably embarrass you and get into trouble. Don't be afraid of therapy or medication. You will be surprised how many people have ADHD or love someone who does. You may have to try several types of medications and doses before you find the kind and amount. Don't be afraid to not medicate your child either. Be honest with your child and tell them what they have. Our son was relieved to know there was a name for why he felt the way he did, and he was happy when he found out his sister and favorite teacher have the same thing and they turned out ok!

I think two qualities a parent must possess when raising children with developmental challenges are flexibility and a sense of humor—not humor at the expense of the child but finding humor in the situation. Both are helpful in diffusing stressful situations. I have noticed, in myself and others, rigidity and an inability to relax at times of heightened stress. The mother's wisdom above to "know that your kids will probably embarrass you and get into trouble" reminds parents to be flexible and face the day with humor. Consider asking yourself before you and your child enter a high-stress situation how your child might embarrass you and how you will remain flexible and respond with humor.

## Be Understanding: Wisdom for Family and Friends

All that parents want family and friends to know about raising children with developmental challenges can be summed up in two words: be understanding. One woman wanted others to know, "I don't consider autism a disability, just a different way of looking at the world." Understanding autism that way frees us from focusing on what is wrong and how to make it right. Then we can get to know the person and learn from them how they understand the world.

> All that parents want family and friends to know about raising children with developmental challenges can be summed up in two words: be understanding.

A mother of two teenage sons with ASD and ADHD explained what she wanted from others was "acceptance. It is not a disease. Be understanding. So often it is just easier to stop seeing other folks than to try and educate them. Folks can be so judgmental." Another parent reiterated this statement, adding, "Stop fucking judging parents. Everyone knows what to do. Except they don't."

Behind this statement, I hear frustration and intense emotion. As we have seen throughout this book, it is tough enough for a parent to wrestle with our own emotions and frustrations raising children with developmental issues. We don't need to hear judgmental comments about our parenting techniques. As one mother simply noted, "It's not our fault." Be understanding of what it is like to parent a child with developmental challenges.

One parent encouraged family and friends "to not be closed minded and ask how they could help. Call us. Encourage us. Maybe offer to help so we get a break." Another parent said, "If you have a friend whose kid has ADHD, support her, listen to her fears, and don't discount them." One mother of a teenage daughter diagnosed with ASD wanted others to know "listening is more helpful than making suggestions; unless you are actually trained in these things, I don't want to hear your theories. There were times [when we asked ourselves] 'What did we do that caused this?' Walking with us through grieving what we expected parenthood to be like would be lovely." Be understanding and supportive of the parents.

Other parents want family and friends to be understanding about the child's disorder. One mother would like "to teach 'normal' children how to treat my ADHD child." Another mother responded, "The child does not 'choose to be bad.' The child's behavior is the best they can do at the time. They don't mean to cause trouble, but they lack certain skills, and punishing them for behavior doesn't teach them those skills." A mother with six adopted children, each with developmental challenges, encouraged others:

Listening is more helpful than making suggestions; unless you are actually trained in these things, I don't want to hear your theories.

Listen with your eyes! If my child is having what appears to be a behavior problem, there is an underlying cause. Let them show you what they need; be open and patient. They want to learn. They want to be accepted and treated equally. Help them find a way they can learn best. Be ready for anything. *Read*, be trained. Help us be able to be included in the community.

Another mother suggested how others could be supportive of her and her daughter:

For adults who interact with my child when she is not medicated—to help them understand how ADHD manifests in my daughter and why medication for evening activities is absolutely *not* an option. I always appreciate learning how other adults experience my child—any insights they might have. Sometimes the best help is a nonjudgmental shoulder to cry on and help to take care of myself and my marriage!

Parents want others to be understanding of their challenges, the child's disorder, and of what is unhelpful. One mother offers all this wisdom in one paragraph:

When people find out my kids have diagnoses, they say, "But they don't look hyper." So unhelpful. Or they begin to wonder if their rambunctious toddler has ADHD (too early to know!). Mostly please just learn who my kid is, what is important to them, and appreciate whatever they bring to the table (which can be challenging at times). Not so different from other kids. I also struggle with the dumb Facebook article that floats around from time to time about how French kids don't get ADHD. I could scream!

As parents, we want you to get to know our child. It is not difficult to do. One does not have to be a trained professional to do this. Care about the child. Talk to them, not about them or at them. By doing this, I can almost guarantee that every parent will thank you.

> As parents, we want you to get to know our child. It is not difficult to do. One does not have to be a trained professional to do this.

## Be Truly Welcoming and Flexible: Wisdom for Faith Communities

One mother succinctly encapsulated the wisdom of all the parents for faith communities when she responded, "Be truly welcoming and flexible. Look for and support the gifts. Don't focus on the difficulties. My child is as valuable as others. He is created in the image of God."

To be welcoming is more than stating on a sign or in a bulletin "all are welcome." A mother of a teenage daughter diagnosed with ASD challenged the statement. She responded, "When we say, 'all are welcome' we need to really mean it, not just 'all neurotypical are welcome.'" Members of faith communities may think they welcome all people, but it takes a concerted effort to extend welcome to people who are different—whether it is race, age, socioeconomic class, gender preferences, or neurologic. The challenge for people in faith communities is to *be* welcoming, to understand welcoming is a verb. Welcoming is an act of openness, understanding, and caring for another person.

One woman shared what welcoming would look like for her and her daughter with autism. "Our child is 'high functioning' and I don't think I should have to share her diagnosis in order to avoid the glares of people at church who openly embrace the children with more obvious diagnoses and behaviors." A young woman who lives with autism told of her experience of attending a faith community, from a young child until now, and how she would like to be welcomed:

> Especially as a kid, I took directions very literally; if the choir director says "stand up" and not "sit down," I'll stay standing (particularly if they've already scared us by being an intimidating person!). Feeling guilt-tripped and hopeless doesn't help me; I don't want to feel miserable from my church.

A mother described her experience with her preschool-aged daughter at her faith community,

Don't focus on the difficulties. My child is as valuable as others. He is created in the image of God.

I wish there was some way for churches to raise awareness of special-needs kids. I don't know how they would do it other than put some weird announcement in the bulletin reminding parishioners that some kids have special needs, but I am so sick of getting dirty looks when my daughter has a meltdown. It helps that she looks younger than she is, and people assume that she's an appropriate age for meltdowns, but I don't know how much longer that's going to last, and even so, we still get dirty looks. I wish that faith communities were more [intentional] about having cry rooms. I get the impulse to say that kids are part of the church community and shouldn't be told to leave, and that if there are cry rooms then parishioners will be scandalized at the presence of a slightly misbehaved child in their midst. I really do. . . . But have a cry room, and for the love of Pete, make it accessible.

Here is more wisdom for members of faith communities:

- "I would ask them for understanding in the challenges of parenting these children. I would ask for help: including my kids in social events, realizing what it took to get my kids out the door and to church, helping me while I sit alone with my kids and they are acting up. I want them to realize that we have to work harder to get our kids to do everyday activities. It is exhausting. Befriend our kids. Give them a reason to want to come to church. ADHD is a medical condition. If my boys had cancer, diabetes, or another medical condition, people would be more sympathetic. It's a very lonely life."

- "It is very difficult to go anywhere, even church. Many people mean well but just don't understand, and I'm not comfortable leaving my child with them without me. *Ask questions!* Each child is different, ask what you can do to help. Don't be afraid of my children! Yes, they may act differently than your child, but they ARE people too. Accept the difference, see them for who they are, not what they do."

- "First, *never, ever, ever tell the child and parent that they don't belong in church and that God doesn't love your child*!!!!!!! I would say to have a place for the parents and kids to feel safe. Offer a place

---

If my boys had cancer, diabetes, or another medical condition, people would be more sympathetic. It's a very lonely life.

for the kids to go so that the parents are able to attend a Bible study and meet other church members. If you see a family struggle, help them. When my son had cancer, people from church helped out, but when my daughter was in the psych unit at the hospital or in residential treatment *no one* helped. We needed help but felt like outcasts! Church is judgmental and hurts! It should be a place to refresh and renew instead of so much pain!"

- "All children are precious, valued, wanted. People with ADHD and ASD can grow up to live productive lives. Even when they can't be 'productive,' they can still be happy and touch other people's lives in real and meaningful ways. They can love others. Through them, they and God can teach us patience, kindness, gentleness, compassion, empathy, and many other character traits. Caring for others makes us better people. Make this world a better place to live in. One of our God-given callings in this life is to be the best mother/aunt/grandma/teacher/church/friend . . . to all people in our midst we are called to care for. Love, have joy, have peace, patience, kindness, goodness, faithfulness, and self-control. Find out and live what God has called you to. And *your* life will be better for you, and better for others. Life can be full of meaning and even joy alongside of its pain, grief, frustrations, and suffering."

Caring for others makes us better people. Make this world a better place to live in.

I hope you hear both the pain and the desire of these parents for them and their children to be welcomed and supported by their faith communities. The experiences and the wisdom gained and offered in this chapter hopefully will encourage parents to "hang in there," help family members and friends to be understanding, and challenge members of faith communities to actively welcome parents and children with developmental challenges.

## For Reflection and Discussion

1 What did you think and feel as you read this chapter?

2 What piece of wisdom shared stood out to you? Challenged you?

3 (Parents) If you were to write an instruction book for family, friends, or faith communities what would you include?

4 (Members of Faith Communities) Does your faith community have a statement that "all are welcome?" Are *all* truly welcome?

5 (Members of Faith Communities) How is welcome acted out in your faith community?

# 8

## Living with Hope

For surely I know the plans I have for you, says the Lord, plans for your welfare and not for harm, to give you a future with hope.
—Jeremiah 29:11

THROUGHOUT THIS book, parents of children with developmental challenges have voiced cries of help, joy, challenge, pain, and faith. We have also shared our wisdom gained from our experience: wisdom to care for self and wisdom to share with other parents, family, friends, and faith communities. The experiences of parents of children with developmental challenges are often stressful, and can be overwhelming at times. We all need hope to face life's trials. How does one find hope for the future in the midst of a present that may look bleak? To live in hope is to live in the present moment *while* looking to a better future.

In the New Testament, a passage from Romans 4 talks about the faith and hope of Abraham and Sarah. Even though they were old, they believed God's promise that they would bear a child and give birth to a nation of people. The problem with the promise was that both Sarah and Abraham were over ninety years old—not prime childbearing years. Paul, the writer of Romans states, "Hoping against hope, [Abraham] believed that he would become 'the father of many nations,' according to what was said, 'So numerous shall your descendants be'" (Rom 4:18). For Sarah and Abraham, "hoping against hope" meant that even when things looked bleak, they still held on to the promises of God. Even though there was no possible way for them to bear a child, they still had hope God would provide them with their own child.

There have been many times in my life I "hoped against hope" God would provide a way where I could not see one. During the first six weeks of our youngest son's life, he was near death. I hoped against hope he would live. When other complications and challenges came, I hoped against hope not only that he would survive but that I would get through it also. This phrase, "hoping against hope," continues to resonate within me after all these years. It conveys persistence, like waves washing up on the shore over and over again. "Hoping against hope" has shaped how I look at hope and how I live with hope.

For me, hope is ultimately holding on to a God who holds on to me, even when I cannot hold on. To live with hope is to face the realities of the present while being held by God and looking to God's unfolding future. Knowing hope can be a powerful force in helping people through challenging times and everyday life, the final question of the survey for the parents of children with developmental challenges was "What gives you hope?"

## Sources of Hope

Hope has many sources. We can place our hope *in* someone or something, like a doctor or education. Or we can have hope *for* something, like a favorable outcome. Or something may *give* us hope, like an encouraging word or test result. The sources of hope may vary, but parents of children with developmental challenges find opportunities for hope.

One mother shared her "hope in God's promises. God made my child beautifully in God's image, and God promises to be with us on this journey."

To live in hope is to live in the present moment *while* looking to a better future.

### In the Child

Parents find hope in the child's innate character or qualities. One mother of a young adult daughter with ASD replied, "She's so incredibly talented and very willing to express her perspective to those who will listen." Another mother said this about her adopted adult son, diagnosed with ADHD and FASD, "He is a kind person, tries very hard to be a good father to his young daughter, and is very loyal." This gave her the hope to add, "We did not fail completely as parents." Here are other qualities parents found in their children that gave them hope:

- "[My son] is bright, capable, and flexible."
- "My child has a beautiful heart and a wonderful capacity for loving everyone regardless of their challenges."
- "[My daughter] is uniquely gifted to offer the world something that isn't typical. Her sensitive heart allows her to have such empathy for those around her."
- "[My older son] is getting more responsible and independent. My younger son is very kind and compassionate."

### The Child Will Be Okay

Parents find hope inspired by the progress their children have made:

- "My children finding happiness and being proud of themselves gives me hope for their future and that one day when I'm not here to help them, they will be ok."
- "They understand what they have (ADHD) and we have worked on ways to play to their strengths. We have talked about the advantages of ADHD, specifically creativity and ability to focus when they are really into something. . . . Our kids really will turn out ok!"

### The Child Is Accepted by Others

A mother of two children with multiple challenges cited "supportive friends" as a form of hope. Hope can also be given by those closest to us, such as family members or spouses, through

God made my child beautifully in God's image, and God promises to be with us on this journey.

their presence, support, encouragement, and love. Another mother found hope that her son "is loved by many people." To be loved and accepted is something all of us want. Parents who have children with developmental challenges deeply desire for our children to be loved and accepted by others. Parents found hope in these situations:

- "My church youth group, which treats him no differently than any other kid."
- "That more folks who are neurotypical have things in common with [my children]. And as they move on to college, they will find others like them to associate with."

### The Child's Milestones and Accomplishments

Parents found hope in their child's milestones or accomplishments—including growth and development. These accomplishments do not need to be big things. Small things like "a very minor accomplishment, a thank you, and their love" are important to them too. Parents found hope:

- "Seeing them mature and meeting smaller milestones. My older son has had the best grades ever during his junior year, and that was after we had to move to another school district."
- "He has gotten involved in the drama department at school with stage crew and loves it. He has found how much he enjoys computers and is in the networking program at school. He is advocating for himself at school when he needs something. And he's looking ahead to college."
- "Sometimes, my daughter will ask some really insightful questions or make statements that indicate that she notices more than I think she does. The insights and moments of clarity are definitely a balm for my weary mom soul."
- "Success breeds more success. I have seen my boys achieve more when they can have success. I love seeing their excitement about achieving something new."

Even the accomplishments of other people with developmental challenges bring hope to parents. Another mother of a young son

Parents who have children with developmental challenges deeply desire for our children to be loved and accepted by others.

Parents found hope in their child's milestones or accomplishments.

with ADHD is able to find hope in "having ADHD [myself] and knowing despite having it success is possible." A parent of a toddler with ASD found hope in "reading success stories" of people with autism.

### Hope for Better Days Ahead

Often the progress of children with developmental challenges is slow. It is one step forward and two or three steps back. If there is progress in one area, there tends to be regression in another area, causing many parents to become discouraged or to lose hope. But there are moments when parents get a glimpse it will not always be like this. One mother described what gives her hope, "He has come a long way, and I hope to continue to see improvement in the future (even if it is slow!)."

I remember vividly the first time we went to a restaurant and our youngest son did not run all over the place. It was at a small take-and-bake pizza restaurant, strategically chosen. When he ran, we could catch him quickly, and he could be entertained by watching the pizza being made. When I entered the restaurant with my son, there was a short line of people waiting to order. I almost considered leaving and coming back in a few minutes. Instead, I took a deep breath to prepare myself for the wait and whatever my son might do. He stood next to me the whole time. It was only a few minutes, but to me it was a small miracle and a major accomplishment! From that day forward, slowly, he could stay still longer and longer until we actually were able to go to sit-down restaurants again and enjoy our meal.

### Hope for a Distant Future

The hope for some parents may be in the distant future. A reality for many parents of children with complex developmental challenges is the hope for a time when the child's needs will no longer be all encompassing. Often, when the child's needs are great, a parent must put their own needs aside for a while to care for the child.

*He has come a long way, and I hope to continue to see improvement in the future (even if it is slow!).*

The length of this time varies from months to years. But hope keeps them going in the face of an uncertain and far off future.

One mother's adopted teenage daughter is not only diagnosed with ASD and ADHD but Huntington's Disease. Huntington's is a terminal degenerative brain disease that, when developed before twenty years old, progresses very fast, resulting in a decline in physical, mental, and emotional capacities. This is a challenging burden. She holds on to the hope that someday her daughter "will be in heaven. And my husband and I will not have her burdens to bear while we are old." While she cares for her daughter, she works on "developing a life for myself apart from my kids so that . . . I will still have . . . God's gifts and calling on my life besides that of motherhood." The future will look very different from the present, and she wants to be prepared for it.

*Hope in External Developments*

A few parents found hope in external developments, such as medication, research, or education. One mother shared:

> My son has just started taking medication [for ADHD] and it makes him so much better—he acts like himself, but like a calm version of himself. He loves being on meds because he's so happy that he can finally be calm. It's only been two weeks, but I'm hopeful that this will finally be what turns things around.

Other parents found hope in research into developmental challenges and using that information to educate other people. A mother of many adopted children said, "Autism research gives me hope for understanding in others." Research has helped inform and more deeply understand developmental challenges, and it has led to education strategies that offer hope. Another mother found hope for her teen sons diagnosed with ASD and ADHD in "the form of social-skills classes." The skills they are learning in these classes are helping them learn and grow, so that someday they will be able to live on their own.

A reality for many parents of children with complex developmental challenges is the hope for a time when the child's needs will no longer be all encompassing.

## When Hope Is Elusive

There may be times in the journey of parenting a child with developmental challenges when a parent has difficulty seeing hope, finding hope, or being hopeful. This can happen after a parent receives the diagnosis and are overwhelmed with emotions and information.

Sometimes hope for parents of children with developmental challenges is elusive. Some children have challenges that will never go away, never lessen, never get better, and the parents struggle to find hope in their situation. One parent answered the survey question "What gives you hope?" with "not much." Another parent answered the question with a one-word question, "Hope?"

When hope is elusive for someone we love, we often try to find hope for them. We cannot impose hope upon others, but we can stay with them and listen. We can use hope to strengthen ourselves, so we may continue to love and support others through difficult times.

*We can use hope to strengthen ourselves, so we may continue to love and support others through difficult times.*

## Living with Hope

Throughout this book, I have contributed my reflections along with the cries, wisdom, and hopes of parents of children with developmental challenges. We have shared our experiences and complex internal emotions as parents. My hope for parents of children with developmental challenges is that they learn they are not alone on this journey. It is a long and incredible journey filled with joys, pains, and love. I also hope family, friends, and members of faith communities gain a glimpse of what this journey is like and develop insight on how they might come alongside parents of children with developmental challenges.

I have often wished for an instruction book for parenting a child with developmental challenges. I thought it would make the journey easier. The journey has been both frustrating and amazing. My heart has been broken with pain and it has overflowed with love. I have often wondered if my parenting has been good enough or if I could have done better. But looking back, I see I have been living with hope all along—even when I didn't realize it. I lived with hope God would strengthen our skills as parents to raise our son in love and faith. I lived with hope God would provide for our son's needs so he could achieve his full potential.

I have been a parent to my son for twenty-three years without an instruction book, but I could not have emerged with my humor intact, a joy of life, and a grateful attitude if not for my relationship with God, family, friends, other parents, and members of the faith community.

What if I could have done better?
  Worked harder.
  Called more people.
  Made a difference for all children.

What did I do today?
  I didn't get the laundry done.
    I didn't make that phone call.
    I didn't follow up with a friend.

What did I do today?
    Loved my child.
    Took a walk.
    Received help from a friend.

What if?
  There is more to parenting than doing stuff?
  I made a difference in someone's life today
  and didn't know it?

What if?
  I gave hope to my child by showing up?
  I don't need to understand hope to live it?

—HHW

Looking back, I see I have been living with hope all along—even when I didn't realize it.

## For Reflection and Discussion

1 What gives you hope?

2 What did you think and feel as you read this chapter?

3 (Parents) How does having hope affect how you parent your children? How does it affect you?

4 (Members of Faith Communities) What Scriptures of hope are important to you? Explain.

5 (Members of Faith Communities) How might your community of faith carry hope for those who find hope elusive?

# Resources

## Disorder-Specific Websites

Autism Society of America (www.autism–society.org)

- The nation's leading grassroots autism organization. Working to increase public awareness about the day-to-day issues of people across the spectrum, to advocate for appropriate services for individuals of every age, and to provide the latest information regarding treatment, education, research, and advocacy.

CHADD (www.chadd.org)

- A national nonprofit organization that improves the lives of people affected by ADHD through education, advocacy, and support. CHADD is in the forefront of creating and implementing programs and services in response to the needs of adults and families affected by ADHD through collaborative partnerships and advocacy, including training for parents and K–12 teachers, hosting educational webinars and workshops, being an informative clearinghouse for the latest evidence-based ADHD information, and providing information specialists to support the ADHD community.

National Organization on Fetal Alcohol Syndrome (www.nofas.org)

- Works to prevent prenatal exposure to alcohol, drugs, and other substances known to harm fetal development by raising awareness and supporting women before and during their pregnancy, and supports individuals, families, and communities living with Fetal Alcohol Spectrum Disorders (FASDs) and other preventable intellectual/developmental disabilities.

## For Parents

Bohager, Tom. "Care for the Caregiver / Self Care." Autism Hope Alliance, May 11, 2017 (https://tinyurl.com/y7fmdry2)

- This article addresses the challenges of self-care for parents who have children with autism. Beginning with the oxygen-mask analogy—putting yours on first before placing one on a young child—the author encourages tending to one's health in a variety of ways and concludes by telling parents to beware of guilt-tripping themselves when they practice self-care.

Bradley, Lorna. *Special Needs Parenting: From Coping to Thriving.* Minneapolis: Huff, 2015.

- This book can be read alone or used in a parent support group. Each chapter offers personal stories, pastoral reflection, and scriptural reflections of the author as well as questions and prayers. The author is a skilled faith-based group facilitator for parents of children with special needs, and her expertise shines on each page. Bradley has a resource list in the back of her book for parents and churches. Below are a few she lists under "Ongoing Special Needs Parent Support":

    Bolduc, Kathleen Deyer. *Autism and Alleluias.* Valley Forge, PA: Judson, 2010.

    Bolduc, Kathleen Deyer. *His Name Is Joel: Searching for God in a Son's Disability.* Louisville: Bridge Resources, 1999.

    Bolduc, Kathleen Deyer. *The Spiritual Art of Raising Children with Disabilities.* Valley Forge, PA: Judson, 2014.

    Philo, Jolene. *A Different Dream for My Child: Meditations for Parents of Critically or Chronically Ill Children.* Grand Rapids: Discovery House, 2009.

CHADD. "For Parents and Caregivers" (https://tinyurl.com /y8jcszjf)

- This article addresses specific ways parents and caregivers can help themselves, and their child with ADHD, succeed.

Friend, Jamie L. "Caregiver Stress: Don't Forget Self-Care." Mayo Clinic (https://tinyurl.com/y8wcfmhd)

- This article lists signs of burnout and what one can do about it as well as self-care tips.

Mayo Clinic Staff. "Caregiver Stress: Tips for Taking Care of Yourself." Mayo Clinic (https://tinyurl.com/y7pc5cdd)

- This article notes the rewarding aspects of caregiving as well as the stressors. Lists signs of caregiver stress and strategies for dealing with it.

Special Learning, Inc. "Caring for the Caregiver" (https://tinyurl.com/ybqgmnlw)

- Specifically for parents who have children with autism. Notes four major points for parents to keep in mind while watching their own stress or anxiety: patience, getting help when needed, sharing, and motivation.

### Websites

The Arc (www.thearc.org)

- The nation's leading advocate for all people with intellectual and developmental disabilities and their families, and the premier provider of the supports and services people want and need.

PACER Center (www.pacer.org)

- A Minnesota-based parent-training and information center for families of children and youth, from birth to young adults, with all disabilities. Offers live-stream events and archived live-stream events on many topics.

Washburn Center for Children. "Resources for Common Family Challenges" (https://tinyurl.com/yauum9c6)

- Helpful tips for parents and family members for common challenges including these topics: children and anxiety, children and grief and loss, children and self-esteem, and children and identity.

## Bullying

PACER's National Bullying Prevention Center (www.pacer.org/bullying)

- Provides resources designed to benefit all students, including those with disabilities.

Stopbullying.gov

- An official website of the United States Government with extensive information on bullying, cyberbullying, prevention, what schools and kids can do, state laws and policies, and more.

Washburn Center for Children. "How to Address Bullying with a Child" (https://tinyurl.com/y9djj2be)

- This article lists practical things parents can do to support and encourage a child who is being bullied.

## For Faith Communities

Carter, Erik W. *Including People with Disabilities in Faith Communities: A Guide for Service Providers, Families, and Congregations*. Baltimore, MD: Paul H. Brookes, 2007.

- A comprehensive guide for leaders of Faith Communities complete with practical strategies and helpful resources. The author writes from a research background but also writes about hospitality, belonging, community, natural supports, and reciprocity.

Christensen, Shelly. *Jewish Community Guide to Inclusion of People with Disabilities*. Minneapolis: Inclusion Innovations, 2012.

- Written specifically for the Jewish community, this resource includes grounding in liturgy and Torah as well as worksheets, assessments, and check lists to attend to the practical matters on including people with disabilities in all aspects of the faith.

Gaventa, Bill, ed. *Dimensions of Faith and Congregational Ministries with Persons with Developmental Disabilities and Their Families: A Bibliography and Address Listing of Resources for Clergy, Laypersons, Families, and Service Providers.* Elizabeth M. Boggs Center on Developmental Disabilities, 2009 (https://tinyurl.com/y96v2jf5)

- Although this resource was developed in 2009, it was the most comprehensive bibliography of the time. With an extensive table of contents and over two hundred pages of resources, it can be a good place to start if looking for something specific.

Lee, Amy Fenton. *Leading a Special Needs Ministry: A Practical Guide to Including Children and Loving Families.* Cumming, GA: Orange, 2013.

- A practical "how-to" handbook that covers care of parents as well as developing programs, policies, and education for volunteers working with children with disabilities in congregations.

Newman, Barbara J. *Accessible Gospel, Inclusive Worship.* Wyoming, MI: CLC Network, 2015.

- Specific guide to creating inclusive worship opportunities, for people with intellectual and developmental disabilities, based on the vertical habits developed by the Calvin Institute of Christian Worship. The vertical habits are praise, confession lament, illumination, petition, gratitude, service, and blessing.

Newman, Barbara J. *Autism and Your Church: Nurturing the Spiritual Growth of People with Autism Spectrum Disorders.* Grand Rapids: Faith Alive Christian Resources, 2006.

- This book offers practical ways to welcome and include individuals with Autism Spectrum Disorder into the full life on the congregation.

Taylor, Courtney E., Erik W. Carter, Naomi H. Annandale, Thomas L. Boehm, and Aimee K. Logeman. *Welcoming People with Developmental Disabilities and Their Families: A Practical Guide for Congregations*. Vanderbilt Kennedy Center, January 2014 (https://tinyurl.com/y8ys6qvj)

- This guide was written to equip congregations with ideas and practical steps to strengthen the invitation, supports, and hospitality offered to people with disabilities and their families.

Thornburgh, Ginny, and Ann Davie. *That All May Worship: An Interfaith Welcome to People with Disabilities*. American Association of People with Disabilities, March 2016 (https://tinyurl.com/y742brem)

- This handbook was first published in 1996 by the National Organization on Disability (NOD). It was the first of its kind to assist congregations in welcoming people with disabilities. This PDF version was updated in 2016. It is a concise guide and a good introduction for members of faith communities who want to welcome all people.

Walsh, Mary Beth, Alice F. Walsh, and William C. Gaventa, eds. *Autism and Faith: A Journey into Community*. Elizabeth M. Boggs Center on Developmental Disabilities and New Jersey Center for Outreach and Services for the Autism Community, May 2008 (https://tinyurl.com/ydarwaah)

- This interfaith booklet contains stories of families and individuals as well as clergy and professionals with autism to help faith communities include people with autism as part of the community.

*Websites*

American Association on Intellectual and Developmental Disabilities Religion and Spirituality Division (www.aaiddreligion. org)

- Resources, networking, and certification for clergy and lay leaders to minister to people with intellectual and developmental disabilities.

Autism Society. "Autism and Faith" (https://tinyurl.com/yb8yrbm7)

- The Autism Society faith initiative intends to create autism-friendly environments in all places of worship.

Collaborative on Faith and Disability (http://faithanddisability.org)

- The mission of the Collaborative on Faith and Disability is to support people with disabilities, their families, and those who support them by providing national and international leadership in the areas of research, education, service, and dissemination related to disability, religion, and inclusive supports.

# Notes

## Introduction: If Only Children Came with Instructions

1. I have chosen not to use the names of my family members throughout this book. I feel using their names draws attention to them. The story I will be sharing is my own; even though it includes them, it is not their story. I want them to be free to tell their own story.

2. The *Diagnostic and Statistical Manual of Mental Disorders: DSM-5* (5th ed. [Arlington, VA: American Psychiatric Association, 2013], 50–59) classifies Asperger's syndrome as an Autism Spectrum Disorder, whereas the earlier version (*Diagnostic and Statistical Manual of Mental Disorders: DSM-IV-TR*, 4th ed. [Washington, DC: American Psychiatric Association, 2000], 80–84) classified it as a separate disorder.

3. Some people with nonverbal autism may be able to communicate through self-directed electronic communication or facilitated communication, which requires another person to facilitate.

4. "FASD," National Organization on Fetal Alcohol Syndrome (NOFAS), https://tinyurl.com/y7cpvg3p.

5. The survey and research process were approved by the Luther Seminary (Saint Paul, MN) Institutional Review Board on May 2, 2017. Of the fifty-nine respondents, thirty-nine completed the entire survey while twenty completed portions of the survey.

## Chapter 1: Something's Not Quite Right: A Cry for Help

1. Reluctant to take food or drink by mouth.

2. This is an ongoing and complex debate. For a brief review, see Daniel Rettew, "The ADHD Debate," *Psychology Today*, January 6, 2014, https://tinyurl.com/yaztvd99.

3. This process is modified from the four tasks of mourning from J. William Worden's *Grief Counseling and Grief Therapy*, 4th ed. (New York: Springer, 2009): to accept the reality of the loss, to process the pain of grief, to adjust to a world without the person you lost, and to find an enduring connection with the person you lost in the midst of embarking on a new life.

## Chapter 3: It Never Ends: A Cry of Challenge

1. "Resources for Common Family Challenges," Washburn Center for Children, https://tinyurl.com/yauum9c6.

## Chapter 4: How Long? A Cry of Pain

1. PACER's National Bullying Prevention Center, www.pacer.org/bullying.
2. "Top 10 Facts that Parents, Educators and Students Should Know," Bullying and Harassment of Students with Disabilities, PACER's National Bullying Prevention Center, 2016, https://tinyurl.com/y8wwkd4a.
3. The Mighty Staff, "New Study Challenges Divorce Stats for Parents of Kids with Disabilities," The Mighty, November 4, 2015, https://tinyurl.com/yc9tprvz.

# Bibliography

American Psychiatric Association. *Diagnostic and Statistical Manual of Mental Disorders: DSM-5*. 5th ed. Arlington, VA: American Psychiatric Association, 2013.

———. *Diagnostic and Statistical Manual of Mental Disorders: DSM-IV-TR*. 4th ed. Washington, DC: American Psychiatric Association, 2000.

"FASD." National Organization on Fetal Alcohol Syndrome (NOFAS). https://tinyurl.com/y7cpvg3p.

The Mighty Staff. "New Study Challenges Divorce Stats for Parents of Kids with Disabilities." The Mighty, November 4, 2015. https://tinyurl.com/yc9tprvz.

National Organization on Fetal Alcohol Syndrome (NOFAS). www.nofas.org.

PACER's National Bullying Prevention Center. www.pacer.org/bullying.

———. "Top 10 Facts that Parents, Educators and Students Should Know." Bullying and Harassment of Students with Disabilities, 2016. https://tinyurl.com/y8wwkd4a.

Rettew, Daniel. "The ADHD Debate." *Psychology Today*, January 6, 2014. https://tinyurl.com/yaztvd99

Washburn Center for Children. "Resources for Common Family Challenges." https://tinyurl.com/yauum9c6.

Worden, J. William. *Grief Counseling and Grief Therapy: A Handbook for the Mental Health Practitioner*. 4th ed. New York: Springer, 2009.